The Mystery of Me

Behind our dark moods
and deep longings,
at the heart of our loves and fears,
is power waiting to be discovered—
and a gentle presence that makes itself felt
through surprises all along the way.

Joe Mannath, S.D.B.

The Mystery of Me

IMAGE BOOKS
DOUBLEDAY
New York London Toronto Sydney Auckland

AN IMAGE BOOK

Published by Doubleday, a division of Bantam Doubleday Dell Publishing Group, Inc., 666 Fifth Avenue, New York, New York 10103

IMAGE, DOUBLEDAY, and the portrayal of a cross intersecting a circle are trademarks of Doubleday, a division of Bantam Doubleday Dell Publishing Group, Inc.

Originally published in India by Chair Publications.
This edition published by special arrangement with the author.

Library of Congress Cataloging-in-Publication Data

Mannath, Joe.
  [You surprised me]
  The mystery of me/Joe Mannath.—1st Image Books ed.
    p. cm.
  Reprint. Originally published: You surprised me. Madras : Chair Publications, © 1987.
  1. Meditations. I. Title.
BX2182.2.M285   1987
242—dc20   89-35092
CIP

ISBN 0-385-26382-1

Dedication

I see the map come alive with sacred places,
places made holy by the touch of friendship.

Friends surprised me, seeing a me I had not seen;
friends challenge me still to come home and explore.

To each of them I say:
Thank you for meeting me
where it matters most to meet;
thank you for opening my eyes
to what I could not see alone.

I dedicate this edition
to my friends in the U.S.,
especially to the parish community
of St. Luke's, Belmont, Massachusetts.

Contents

SPECIAL PERSONS

SPECIAL OCCASIONS

EVERY DAY, EVERY NIGHT

HOW DO I PICTURE YOU?

YOU SURPRISED ME

QUESTIONS PEOPLE ASK

Foreword

Whoever said, "What is most intimate, is most universal," was not playing with words.

The writing of this book and the reactions of readers have convinced me that the statement is profoundly true.

Recalling the touching breakthroughs I had witnessed in counseling and therapy sessions, and using the freeing truths learnt from a few remarkable friends, from academic work, and from silence, I tried to put into words some of the anguish and the ecstasy I glimpsed in the human heart. I attempted to trace inner journeys to serenity, accessible paths that start right at our doorstep.

As the manuscript made the rounds among friends of eight different nationalities and very different backgrounds—teachers and teenagers, couples and celibates, professionals and housewives—a common pattern of response emerged.

"You have described me," was a frequent comment. "This is exactly how I feel," others said. Not a few remarked, "There is intimacy here. These are the things I feel, and think about, and wish I could put into words."

Healing was another theme the responses frequently touched upon—the experience of peace and healing, as one looked into one's pain and confusion, one's loves and longings.

Others said they welcomed a free and freeing type of

prayer—a prayer shorn of pious jargon, in touch with one's feelings and questions.

I want to thank the men and women who walked with me—or led me—towards the truths that set me free. They are present in the pages that follow—through their inspiration, their love, their example, their confrontation, their listening, their zest for life. A few of them are mentioned under "Memories Behind the Words"; there are, however, many more who helped me to search and to find.

With pleasure, therefore, and with gratitude, I recall my professors at the Salesian University, Rome, especially my doctoral guide, Professor Prospero T. Stella, S.D.B.; my senior tutor at Oxford, Reverend Vincent Turner, S.J.; my counselors and spiritual directors over the years, in particular Fathers M. M. Balaguer, Thomas Panakezham, Matt Altrichter, Dick McHugh and William Connolly; Carlos Welch; the late Anthony DeMello of Sadhana Institute; the men and women who have opened their hearts to me, showing me time and again that those who seek help often give it without realizing it.

Some of the most significant persons who helped me to open my eyes and see what I write about cannot be mentioned by name; so, let me tell them: to you, who have loved me enough to stand by me, and trusted me enough to confront me, I dedicate this book.

Coming to the writing itself, I am happy to thank a number of special people:

The parish community of St. Luke's, Belmont, Massachusetts, especially its gracious pastor, Reverend Richard J. Powers, whose hospitality made the writing of this book—and other tasks I was engaged in—more a privilege than a chore; George and Edith Williamson, Stephen and Susannah Garrity, and Sr. Doris Lambert, who read the manuscript and made valuable suggestions; Mary Lally, Mary Grace and Anne Shaw, who so efficiently deciphered, typed, and retyped what I wrote; other friends who prodded and pushed, when I needed pushing and prodding, and in many ways made my stay in Belmont a "coming-home" experience.

Back in India, friendship showed itself in the form of cheerful and generous help: Professor Thomas George, who took up the publication; Kurien and Rebecca Kattikaren, who saw to many of the practical details with characteristic and self-effacing efficiency; Gina Hanna, who read the proofs; Giuliano Santi and his hardworking team at the Siga Press, who went beyond the call of duty to produce a work of quality.

So much kindness; so many surprises all along the way.

Friends have done more than help me write a book. They "got me hooked" on the most fascinating book of all—the mystery of the human being.

The human being I am, the human being you are; the fallible, fascinating riddle we are right now.

No wonder the map comes alive with precious memories . . .

JOE MANNATH, S.D.B.
Belmont, Massachusetts • Madras, India

Memories Behind the Words

The young man from France was curious. Here was a thin, old man, seated on a matted palm leaf by the bank of the river. The river was the Cauvery in South India. The old man turned out to be a wise and good Moslem, and my friend and I listened to his story.

It was a common enough story: a famished boy who worked as a servant, traveled with his rich boss and was promised the fare for his life's dream, a trip to Mecca. What made the story different was also what it taught me about the meaning of pilgrimage. For the old man of my story gave up his chance to go to Mecca (every Moslem's lifelong dream) to let someone else go in his place. "We should not be greedy in these matters," he said, convinced that God would find him anywhere, provided his heart was ready.

There are many other "angels in disguise" who taught me the essential things of life in simple ways. Shall I venture to fill these minutes with a few sacred memories?

The radiance of Tonino, a badly crippled teenager I met at a youth rally near Naples. He was unable to talk, and could hardly hold a pencil. Strapped in a wheelchair, he coaxed twisted fingers into writing a note to his youth group. It was a greeting of pure joy. "We must not refuse God anything," was the heart of the message. As we read the page with moist eyes, Tonino looked around us with unconcealed happiness.

Roberta, who communicates such serenity and warmth, and an incredible understanding of the human heart, as we write to each other, or talk through the grill of her Clarist cloister in Milan. Prayer puts her in touch with "the essentials," as she says, and gives her a vision that comes straight from the heart. No wonder shopkeepers and college students, parents and street people, are drawn to confide in this woman, whose choice of life they do not understand.

The men and women I have met on reflection days or in prayer groups—in India, in Rome, in England, in the United States—many of whom are so much more alive than they were before. As they moved from conventional religion to depth, from pious jargon to honesty, they became more real—and more fun to be with.

Hindu Monks in Rishikesh, on the banks of the river Ganges, welcoming pilgrims from anywhere and celebrating both Diwali and Christmas in a spirit of God-given brotherhood.

Andrew and Josephine, who gave up lucrative careers to live and work with the poor, showing me both the dynamism of love ("orthopraxis," they called it) and the dignity of human beings. They also exposed the cowardice and incoherence behind some of my positions. It is more comfortable to talk than to take seriously the human reality that learning and religion refer to.

Spiritual directors and masters—Catholic and Protestant, Hindu and Sikh—who taught me to look within. The light comes from within—and dispels the dangerous myth that others are less godly than our group. How can God be God and ask us to behave as competing groups?

The sparkle in the eyes of an old Swiss woman of Lugano, as she sang in her pastry shop, stopping in between to tell me: "We must not be afraid of death." She was not.

The look in my father's eyes as he knelt before the picture of Jesus crowned with thorns. The integrity and compassion which others saw in him; the unworthiness he himself felt.

My mother's resilience and strength. The joyful communities I have lived in, formed by faith, nourished by prayer.

The teachings of Don Bosco, that incomparable friend and teacher of youth. (Keep prayer simple! Our prayer life is not seen during prayer. It is seen in our spontaneous comments and reactions.)

But all is not roses. Side by side with the beauty of lives transformed by faith and goodness, stands the hardening of human hearts made self-righteous in belief. Hatred raised to the honor of religious dogma.

Killings in India. Bombs in Ulster. Crusades in the Middle Ages. Human sacrifices. Men and women burnt at the stake.

All in the name of God. In the name of a good and merciful God.

Poor God!

No, poor us!

We seek divine sanction for our stupidity. We call God in to support our cowardice.

But we are not incurably stupid. We are capable of greatness. We are more than we realize.

God waits to be born in us.

And He will—provided we do not worship our fears.

Provided we do not hide behind a hard shell of prejudice.

For when we wear an armor, it is from love we are protecting ourselves.

In the search for greater love, in the courage to look at ourselves honestly, we have a chance to become human.

The mystic's heart is more human—not more sectarian.

One of the few valid signs—if any—of psychological maturity and growing nearness to God is our expanding sense of self. The "we" in our awareness (and in our conversation) expands to include more and more people, new and different groups. Finding one's identity as someone special who does not need to prove one's importance, the thinking-praying person begins to feel more and more at home everywhere, with anyone.

For our underdeveloped consciousness, mankind is still a motley of warring tribes—not the human family we claim to belong to. While we seek external, structural answers to our divisions, we can also take time for a most practical remedy: finding our God-given identity and worth as human beings.

This is the human—and humanizing—task of reflection and prayer; it is not the prerogative of any group.

If I were asked to point out the world view behind these pages, it would be this:

There is a love which we need not win and cannot lose, a love that is more powerful than human frailty, malice or despair. Not only is this love real; it is the vibrant heart of reality. Given a chance—that is, our assent to look up and to look in—love can take us beyond fear, and transform our halting pace into a flight to the stars. We are meant to fly, not just float.

Silence means making space for this truth.

Prayer is letting the truth transform us.

Growth or maturity implies exposing oneself to the radiance that lies behind words like "I," "We," "Life," "Love," "Pain," "Death."

If you think this sounds like a puzzle—well, in a way, it is.

It is a beautiful puzzle.

On some days it is more puzzling than beautiful.

But, all in all, it is more beautiful than puzzling.

Much more beautiful.

Needs and Moods

In Times of Worry

I am worried.

I do not know whether my fears have a base,
but I tend
to imagine the worst,
and frighten myself.

At times,
without even noticing it,
I find myself tense and self-absorbed,
full of fearful fantasies.

At other times,
I tell myself that I worry too much—
but carry on worrying just the same.
I fear that others will not understand or like me,
if I tell them what is really on my mind.
My words sound foolish even to myself,
as I try explaining.

I wish I could unload my worries
on to a loving shoulder.
I wish I knew what peace and serenity mean.

I realize now
that I am talking to someone
who knows me through and through.
You know everything about me
before I even say it.
You know my inmost secrets,

my deepest needs,
and the very sources of my worry.
You know fully well how I hurt myself,
and what I need to do to be healed.

You are my God, my Mother,
my Father, my one unfailing Friend.
I thank You for being my All.
I thank You for this moment's wisdom.

And I ask You—though I need not even ask—
for the light to see what I do not see,
for eyes that see me as You see me,
for the wisdom to take hold of Your hand.

In Your arms I am totally secure,
whatever may happen to me.
In Your eyes I am precious and beloved,
whatever sores I may carry.
And by Your grace I can face myself
and slay the dragons of my fantasy.

With You at my side,
I am going to look at my worries;
for my time is too precious,
and my life too short,
to be spent—to be wasted—on worry.

When I Feel Lonely

I feel lonely—so terribly lonely.
How gladly I would run away from this—
this aching void,
this painful longing
to reach out and touch someone,
and to be touched.

I know
that I have to face these moments,
that others cannot fill my cup to the brim.
But it is painful, at times really frightening.

There are days when I feel utterly lonely
and nights which I dread facing alone.
I distract myself with work,
with pleasure, with noise.
I seek contact; I try for attention.
I force myself to put on a brave smile—
but the pain remains.
The empty hours drag on,
followed by more empty hours.

My heart is thirsty.
I feel like a barren wasteland,
giving nothing, getting nothing,
meaning nothing to anyone.
Help me through the desert,
for I do not see the way.
I have dragged myself to mirage after mirage,

and felt cheated each time.
And yet I find myself rushing
to the next false oasis.

Help me to look into myself.
Show me what I need, and how to find it.
Show me where You hide and wait for me—
and that will be enough for me.

I will not wander far, hungry and thirsty,
while You offer me good food and drink in plenty.
You have made me so great—
too great for this world,
too deep to be filled by trifles.
Fill my lonely heart as You alone can.
Speak to my heart in words You alone can utter.

I wait before You in silence.
Here is my little bowl, battered and empty.
Fill it to the brim as You alone can!
Fill it to overflowing!

If this pain, this emptiness,
has shown me the way to You,
I am more than glad You let me feel it.
For You are the fullness my lonely heart aches for,
and, when I find You, I am speechless with joy.

When I Feel Depressed

No one will know how dark my nights are.
No one understands the weight on my heart.

I fret, I withdraw, I find life a burden,
an almost unbearable burden.
I wish I too could smile from my heart.
I too long for peace and for strength and courage.
I dread being alone;
and I fear talking to others.
Both solitude and company hold their special terrors.

My fantasies are frightening; I dare not utter them.
I wonder: am I going crazy?
Oh God, what is happening to me?
What has happened to joy and pleasure and hope
and the thrill of being close to people?
How do I get out of this frightening gloom,
this dark tunnel with no light in sight?

I need You now,
as I've never needed You.
I need to believe You are there.
No, I need to feel You close.
Faith seems too vague a word
and human assurances feel empty.
Can You fill my heart today,
and lift me out of the pit?
From my hidden dangers, save me!

From the night of my depression,
release me! Set me free!

Break through these walls,
for I feel like a frightened child.
Take me by the hand and lead me to the light.
Take away the demons of my fantasy
and the dark, nameless terrors I dread.
Turn my weeping into joy!

May this suffering teach me
compassion and tenderness,
and give me a listening heart.
May it soften me and make me gentle,
ever willing to forgive,
and slow to condemn.

May it purify me of my selfishness and my hardness
of heart.
May it make me more like You.
May I learn to weep not just for my sorrows,
but for the pains of humanity,
for the many who suffer more than I do.

In my struggles,
never allow me to lose faith in You;
never let me be separated from Your love.
Even in my darkest moments,
may the light of Your face shine upon me,
and bring me peace and comfort.
This I ask as Your child, as Your frightened and
lonely child.

Come soon!
Wipe away my tears! Heal my heart!
Set me free!
In Your will is my peace.

When I Am Angry

I feel so upset, so angry,
almost out of control;
I'm afraid of what I may do.

I didn't know I could be so angry;
I'm surprised at the depth of my feelings.
My whole body feels consumed by rage;
I sweat, I shake, my voice trembles.

I cannot hide behind nice little words,
or put on a nice, pleasant smile.
I wish I could give vent to my anger—
or turn away and scream to my heart's content.

All I can bring before You now
is my anger, this hot consuming rage,
and my struggle to keep this madness in check.

At least with You
I need not pretend to be calm,
or deny the red-hot messages in my head.
I need not try to impress You
with sweet and pious words,
or expect to be told, "Don't be upset!"

For I *am* upset,
more upset and annoyed than I can say,
more angry than I can put into words.

Accept me, please, as I am,
as You have accepted hotheaded humans before me.
Soothe my wounds and heal me!
Protect me from hurting others or myself,
and save me from foolish decisions.
Keep Your loving hand on me—
even when I seem to reject it—
and please wait with me
till I am calm and serene again.

Thank You for meeting me where I am,
for loving me as I am.
Thank You for accepting everything—
my anger, my confusion,
my tears, my guilt.

Hold me and heal me in Your great compassion!
Make my heart gentle and calm.
Make it like Your own.

In Anxiety

Put Your loving arms around me,
and tell my troubled heart to be still.
Do not let my anxious flutter
drown the gentle whisper of Your love.

I need You, my strength,
I need You.

I do not know how to begin,
or even what to say.
One thing I know,
one thing my whole being tells me:
I am anxious, troubled, restless.
My heart is heavy,
my body tense, my hands cold and sweaty.
My speech is rushed,
trying to say a hundred things at once.
I want to rush here and there,
reach out to all the answers I need,
and find the peace my inmost being craves for.

Tell my heart to be still.
Let me relax in Your presence.
May my mind and body—
every fiber of my being—
be softened by the gentle showers of Your mercy.

I do not know what I need;
You do.

In my anxious search I fret and fume,
and run around in circles,
while You wait silently nearby,
infinitely patient, eager to help me,
and with a power beyond my need.

You are at the heart of the storm,
the unshakable tower of strength
where I can take shelter.
Hold me tenderly for a while,
and teach my heart to be still.

Wait with me and calm my anxious mind,
until I am flooded with Your peace.
May Your peace soothe me, fill me, heal me,
and make me radiant with joy.

On a Sleepless Night

I cannot sleep tonight.

I toss about in bed,
and worry about my sleeplessness.
I would give anything for a good night's rest.

The night seems endless.
The minutes feel like hours,
and the hours drag on, heavy with fatigue.
I am exhausted.
I feel restless.
I would give anything in exchange for sleep.

And yet I realize
that there is a purpose even in this;
that nothing happens to me by chance.
I believe that every moment of my life
is present to You—
every minute of this long night,
every moment of every night.

I realize, too, that I see my hours as empty,
if they are not filled with activity.
I become restless if I am not in control.
My annoyance at my sleeplessness
hurts me more than the loss of sleep.

I do not know, my God,
all the reasons for this seemingly endless night.
I do not know all the secrets of my body and mind.

I do not want to run from this.
I want to learn more about myself,
more about life,
more about the apparently useless hours.

In these hours, too, Your love waits for me,
and You are never far away.
What is it You want to tell me tonight?
What are You telling me through my body,
through my restlessness,
through my heavy wakefulness?

Are You asking me to open my heart
to those who suffer on a bed of pain,
to those who work at night at heavy, monotonous
    jobs,
to those whose nights are filled
with anxiety for the morrow?

I'll make room in my heart for You and for them.
I'll learn to relax in Your presence.
I accept both sleep and wakefulness from Your mercy.

I offer up my nights and my days to You.
Give me the grace
to watch with You over the world You love.

Awake or asleep,
may I be a channel of Your love,
and may Your wise and loving plans
be fulfilled in me.

The Mystery of My Body

I want to talk to You about something
that I cannot ignore or entirely remake—my body.
My body has been a source of pleasure and pain,
of worry and pride,
a source of embarrassment and thrills.

Its incredible complexity
is something I take for granted—
until some little part begins to bother me a bit.

I marvel when I hear
that the most complex part of Your creation
is my brain;
that my eyes are far more intricate
than all man-made wonders,
that the tiniest cell in my body
contains untold secrets;
that we have hardly begun
to understand how we are made.

I think of the pleasures I have experienced
through my body—
the taste of food, the beauty of nature,
the feel of things, the closeness of others;
gentle care and reassuring warmth;
and intimate tenderness
without the need for words.

I think also
of the hungers and longings I have known—
the ache of parting, the fatigue after work,
the pain of illness and injury.

I recall my doubts and worries:
Do I look nice?
Am I attractive?
Am I too tall, too short, too fat,
too lean, too dark, too fair . . . ?
Am I losing my charm as I age?
How will I face pain?
And the worry I seldom mention:
how will I die?

Creator and Friend,
everything in me speaks of Your wisdom and love.
Every fiber of my being is Your gift to me.
Nothing in me—or in others—is bad or ugly,
except for eyes without love.
There is no path to You except through my body,
no truth but what I grasp as a bodily being.

These hands that hold this paper,
these eyes, this face,
are the favored sacraments of Your love,
a love that came to me first—and perhaps best—
through other bodies and mine:
my mother's breast,
hands that held me,
arms that sheltered me,
eyes that looked into mine,
lips that uttered words of love . . .

Teach us to reverence our body
and be responsible in its care.
May we never slight or reject anyone
because of their bodies.

May we love our body in all its seasons,
and lovingly nurture it as long as we can.
At last, when our earthly journey is over,
help us to let go of our body gracefully and gratefully,
to prepare for a union
closer than all bodily embraces,
for a life far fuller than the one we know.

Facing My Sexuality

I want to thank You for this gift
which affects me deeply and totally—
my sexuality.

Never for a moment do I stop being sexual.
Even when I would pretend
that I am "above" needs and feelings,
my whole being reminds me—
gently or not so gently—
that I am sexual,
deeply and beautifully sexual.

I have suffered guilt and shame,
embarrassment and fear,
imagining that I was strange,
when I was just being human.

I have blamed myself for feelings and pulls
which came unasked
and shook me out of my apparent calm.
I tended to think—perhaps with millions of others—
that these problems were peculiar to me;
others seemed so poised, so calm, so unsexual.

Thank You for creating me
through the tender passion
of a man and a woman.
Thank You for our sexual nature
that makes us intimately related—

mothers and fathers, brothers and sisters,
adoring grandparents and huggable little children.
So much of the poetry of our humdrum lives
flows from our sexual nature.

Thank You for this divine magic
which pulls us out of ourselves,
and makes us present to one another
intensely, tenderly, and passionately.

May we never sully Your gift
through crude or violent conquest.
May we never reduce the beauty of passion
to the level of a degraded joke.
And may we never, never pretend
that we are more than human.

Help us to accept ourselves as men and women,
see our beauty and our woundedness,
and express our love in passionate tenderness.
Open our eyes
to the beauty of sexuality,
the mystery of human love,
the power and fragility of all that is human.

All Your gifts are beautiful,
and it is worth paying a price
for what is so precious and so life-giving.

We have more to celebrate than we realize;
for in the intensity of sexual longing
and the ecstatic wonder of our love,
You not only grace our lives with a million-colored
    rainbow;
You invite us to be touched by Your own love for us—
Your own passionate, creative love for us.

Falling in Love—Being in Love

How to tell You, oh, how to speak,
of the ecstasy that fills me,
of the heavenly joy I feel,
as I find myself in love and feel so deeply loved!

I know now what it means to be alive!
I have energies I never knew before.
I feel both strong and tender.

Love has shown me the beauty of tears,
the dignity of my body,
the pain of separation,
the ache of longing, and
the ardor of passion.

Oh, how good it is to be alive,
and to let love fill me and guide me!

I never knew I could carry another in my heart
and feel someone's presence so intensely,
without effort and without fatigue.
I never knew I could ache for another's pain
as much as for my own—or even more.

I feel treasured and cared for.
I feel a new aliveness,
a new reverence for myself.
I am in love with life,
close to all that lives,
and closer than ever to You.

I feel like singing;
I feel like shouting;
I am left speechless when I try to talk.
I feel healed of a thousand hurts.
I have seen fears giving way to confidence,
and adolescent awkwardness replaced by tenderness.

Thank You
for making me capable of such love.
Thank You for the beauty we have discovered in each
    other—
the sparkle in the eye,
the little gestures of tenderness,
the warm glow on the face,
the radiance that comes from within.

Thank You for all that we love with—
our hearts and minds, our bodies, our passion,
our gestures and words, and, above all,
the gift of wonder and forgiveness.

Your saints—
far greater lovers than we—
have told us
that all our love
is but a little ray of Your divine light;
that our human ecstasy is only a small,
small reflection of You.

Tiny though it be compared to Your splendor,
what a lovely ray it is,
and what unspeakable beauty it has shown me!

Thank You, Divine Lover, thank You!
Having awakened my heart through love's tender
    touch,
lead me to the unending ecstasy for which You
    created me.

In the Face of Deep Longings

I come to You today less than willingly,
for I feel torn asunder.

I feel these deep, deep urges,
these silent voices of my own needs.
I see that I am pulled in more directions
than I would have thought possible.
I hear the raging seas
that are as much a part of me
as the calm exterior others see.
I see that passion and longing
and weakness and guilt
are a real part of who I am.

My passions seem stronger
than my resolutions.
My hungers seem truer than my polite words.

I escape all clever definitions;
I am not any one of my roles.
I seem a frustrating bundle of contradictions
even to myself.
My longings touch the heavens,
and sound the depths of my most secret desires.
My fascinations are too many to name
or to number.

I wonder if I will ever sort out
the tangled threads of my life,

or stop wishing I were someone else.
Will I ever find someone
who can answer my numberless questions?
I long to see the face of a healer
who will take away my confusion,
make me feel good about myself,
and tell me who I really am.

You are that healer.
For You, I hold no surprises.
Nothing in me shocks You, or puts You off.
All that I feel or dream,
or even fear to look at,
takes on a new beauty in Your eyes.

For You made me
and everything in me.
And You are never ashamed
of what Your hands have made.
Help me to love me
as You love me—
with a patient and forgiving love,
with serenity and humor.

And slowly, under Your gaze,
I will see the truth—
that You made me wonderfully well,
and everything in me
is precious and beautiful.

Thank You, Divine Designer,
for making me what I am—
the wonderful, challenging mystery
You love to hide in.

In Pain or Illness

Help me, O God,
and give me strength,
for I am sick and in pain.

I feel so weak, so tired,
I have no energy for anything.

This sickness has shown me
my need of others,
and the unpredictable turns my life can take.
My health is Your gift,
an undeserved grace I take for granted
till I fall sick or hurt myself.

Thank You for health of mind and body.
Thank You for my strong limbs,
my memory,
my senses,
my bodily and spiritual powers.

I praise You also
for my occasional bouts with illness and pain.

Someone who is in great pain is seldom able to say prayers or "feel devout." The "prayer" in this case—the cry going up to God—is precisely the person's pain or anguish.

What people in pain need is our warm human presence, our loving touch, our delicate attention—not pious lectures or tiring prayers.

Short, simple prayers recited with the suffering person may help—provided it is done in a setting of love and genuine concern.

The prayer given here is meant for sick people who are not in agonizing pain, persons who are well enough to read and to think.

They teach me to appreciate Your gifts
and to understand the sick and the aged.

Give me serenity and strength
that I may bear pain without bitterness,
face sickness without discouragement,
and accept the care of others with simplicity and
    grace.

May I not be a difficult, hard-to-please patient,
or a hypochondriac counting symptoms and never
    getting well.
Teach me to do what I can to help myself,
and to leave to others what they can do better than I.

I offer up to You
my pain, my loneliness, my anxicty.
Give me strength; give me comfort; do not leave me
    alone!

I pray for those who suffer more than I do,
for patients without family or friends,
for the terminally ill and the dying,
for the sick without doctors and nurses,
and for the poor who cannot afford what they need.

Bless me
and all those who look after me,
and dear ones who worry about me.
Bless the generous men and women
who invent medicines or produce them,
or work behind the scenes to make me get better.

May my illness and the care I receive
make me compassionate and human.
May they teach me

to use my health to do the good I can,
and to let go and rest when I need to.

Give me strength, and heal me!
Give me peace!
Bring me healing in body and soul!

Before a Decision

I come to You now
in a moment of confusion,
not knowing what I should do.

I appreciate the trust You place in me,
letting me take decisions,
make mistakes,
be responsible for my life.

At times, however, the burden is crushing,
the possibilities confusing,
the questions too many
and the answers too few.

This is such a moment.
I'm afraid of taking a wrong turn;
I fear the consequences of a misguided decision.
I do not want to hurt others,
or to be hurt—
and I fear appearing less than perfect!

Guide my mind that I may see
what is best for everyone concerned,
and do it with courage
and with love.
Free me from prejudice and from paralyzing fears.
Open my eyes to answers
that I do not yet see.

You see a thousand possibilities where I see none;
You offer me light when I grope in the dark;
You are my tower of strength when I feel frightened.

May Your gentle, unerring light
guide me on the right path.
May it guard me from endless hesitation
and reckless decisions.
May I not rush in
when I need to be cautious,
or wait for perfect conditions
that will never be realized.

Teach me to look with Your eyes,
clasp Your hand,
and take the decisions I need to take today
with humility and courage,
with good sense and wisdom.

May Your wisdom supply what I lack,
and lead me from darkness to the light that I seek.

Wisdom I Seek!

Wisdom I need—
not just cleverness or shrewd common sense,
or the saleable skills of the marketplace.

Wisdom!
Your own wisdom!
A discerning mind and a well-directed heart
to put first things first,
to seek what is worth having,
to fight for what is worth fighting for,
and to rise above daily trifles.

I do not know
the reach of my mind,
nor the endless horizons of my heart.
You who made me,
You whom I unknowingly seek,
it is You who can instruct and guide me.

May Your light fill my mind and heart
that I may see rightly,
judge wisely,
and act effectively.

Save me from arrogance
and hardness of heart!
Protect me from hidden dangers,
from scheming enemies
and from my own blindness.

Make me open to the truth,
amenable to correction,
and docile before counsel.

Do not let me become
a slave of my passions
or a prey to flattery and deceit.

Right now, at this moment,
may Your infinite wisdom come down on me,
and make me wise and strong.

Tell me:
What do You want me to do?
What is the best thing I can do right now?

When Frightened and Nervous

I feel so nervous.

I feel it here in the pit of my stomach,
in my head, in my skin,
in this disconcerting tightness.

As I try to pretend
that I am perfectly in control,
this nagging voice whispers
the most disturbing thoughts.

My overworked fantasy
paints pictures of failure,
scenarios of shame where everyone laughs at me.
"They make me nervous," I say;
"I can't face it."

Behind my tension are my fears,
as You very well know.
Behind the nervous discomfort
stands my raw insecurity.

I am afraid of failure.
I dread making mistakes.
I imagine I will be less than perfect,
that others will laugh at me—
and *that* I cannot face.

How easily I forget
that I am only human,

that it is perfectly OK
to be imperfect.

I imagine others as implacable critics,
ready to pounce on me without pity.
I forget that these others
are as frightened as I am,
in need of kindness,
longing to be affirmed.

I sense dimly, in my better moments,
that it is I who frighten myself.
I let my imagination
paint pictures of doom,
and, before I realize it,
I take them for facts.

I forget my strengths
and the goodness of people,
and their need to be loved by me.
They are hungry, while I think them harsh—
hungry for the very things I too need badly.
They are too busy with their own problems
to be intent on pulling me down.

How easy it is to forget all this!
And how easily I lose sight
of my greatest source of peace and strength—
Your loving gaze which never leaves me,
even for a single instant.

You wait for me in every situation.
You are there in everyone I meet.
You never leave me without the help I need,
or ask me to cross rivers too deep for me.
And so,
when I fret and frighten myself,

steady my mind
and give me wisdom.

May I sense the power of Your presence,
and believe in myself and in those around me.
May I never run away from the good I can do
because of fear and the doubts I carry.
You wait for me in every new setting,
and You will give me all that I need.

What more do I need?

Asking God's Pardon

Forgive me and heal me
in Your tender compassion,
for I have sinned.

I have fallen lower than I like to admit.
I do not know how low I would have fallen,
had not Your grace prevented it.

Reach out to me in Your tender mercy,
and heal me.
Give me a clean heart, a new heart—
a heart like Your own.

I ask Your pardon
for not listening to Your voice,
for not respecting myself,
and for causing suffering to others.

I am guilty of not loving as I should
and as much as I can.
I have turned away from the neighbor who needed
    me,
and refused to share the gifts You have given me.

Forgive me in Your love
for the good I have not done,
and for the evil I have caused.
I ask Your pardon especially for this failure,
which disturbs my conscience . . .

Keep me, my good and loving Saviour,
from a brash denial of my faults
and from an abject contempt for myself.

However faultless I may think I am,
I am far from perfect.
Large spaces in my heart
are still dark and arid.

At the same time,
I am never worthless or beyond hope,
for I am precious in Your eyes,
and Your love is stronger than my sins.

Before You,
I need not defend or excuse myself.
You forgive me, because You love me.
Help me to see the royal beauty
that lies beneath my sins—
a beauty You have given me,
and which I often forget.

May my repentance show me Your face.
May it show me my true worth—my worth as You
    see it.

Sinful, yet loved,
I will sing Your praise;
for You are love,
and nothing I do—or fail to do—
can make You stop loving me.

When Unjustly Treated

I did not deserve this.
I recoil at the way I have been treated.
I did not expect that people I trusted
would turn against me.

This is a bitter pill to swallow,
a very bitter pill indeed.
I take my pain to You,
as well as my anger,
my frustration and my powerlessness.
At least You are always fair and just.
I only get from You what I deserve.

Oh, no, my God,
what have I just said?
Do not treat me as I deserve, for I would die!

You are just,
but not in the punishing little ways I know.
Your justice is another name
for Your steadfast kindness.
You remain faithful and full of tenderness,
even when we are faithless.
You give me far, far greater gifts
than I ever deserve.

How dare I notice only the unjust act
which I think violates my right?
How easily I forget

that I am constantly treated
far beyond my merit!

For Your love is an ocean of mercy
that never runs dry.
Your gifts to me, seen and unseen—
who can count them?
You have loved me through so many people,
many more than I remember.
Even today, as I go about my tasks,
most people are kind and thoughtful,
willing to help, ready to smile.
Thank You, my good and generous God,
for their goodness—and Yours.

Against the vast horizon of so much goodness,
the hurt I have received is small.
It is real, it does affect me,
and I smart from the pain.
But it is a pebble, not a mountain.
It is a wound I can handle.

May this pain teach me thoughtfulness
and make me wise, not bitter.
Behind my hurt,
I see the Loving Hand
that disciplines me, and makes me strong.
Make me strong and noble,
that I may pass from self-pity to joy.
May my wounds never blind me
to the needs of the truly wounded—
or to the surpassing beauty of life.

May nothing I suffer close my heart
to the beauty of flowers,
or the goodness of people—
or to my own capacity to harvest joy
from this field of pain.

In Sadness

What I bring before You today
is my sadness.
I feel it like a stone crushing my heart,
a choking, heavy burden.

My tears—who will understand them?
My sorrow—who will take it away?
Be with me and do not leave me,
for I feel helpless and alone.

I need more than kind words,
far more than words of pity.
I need strength, I need hope,
I need a bit of sunshine.

The world has suddenly become
a frightening, lonely place,
and I feel lost and alone.
Help me, hold me, be with me, please!
Give me again the joy of Your presence.

Help me to believe, even when I do not see.
Help me to hope, though I feel desperate.
Help me never to lose sight of You
and Your tender love.

Lift this heavy burden
from my weak and frightened heart.
You, who are light, joy, love unending,
give me joy,

give me light,
make me feel Your love.

I believe You are near me,
even though I do not see You.
Whatever You do is for my good,
but I do not understand it.
I believe everything has a purpose—
a wise, loving purpose—
though I feel too small to grasp it.

May I hold on to You
in this time of trial
and come out of it
stronger and happier.

Right now, in my writhing anguish,
be near me as never before!
Comfort me, please!

Comfort me with Your tender mercy
until I see the light again.

Learning to Forgive

Of all the divine gifts
that make me like You,
the most divine is this:
that I can forgive,
and be stronger than evil.
I can rise above my anger,
without denying it,
and choose to forgive,
though I cannot forget.

You do not ask me to pretend;
both You and I know my anger.

You do not demand
that I deny my feelings.
You ask me to forgive,
as I myself am forgiven—
constantly and generously forgiven.

You have forgiven and healed me
times without number.
If I were to be treated as I deserve,
I would not exist.
My very life is Your gift to me,
pure, undeserved grace that I constantly receive.

I have fallen more times than I remember,
many more times than I admit.
I have received loving pardon,

both from You and from others.
Who am I, then, to sit in judgement
on my brothers and sisters?
Who am I to decide what each one deserves?

But there are angry days
when I feel revengeful,
when I would gladly lash out,
and hurt those who hurt me.

There is more anger in me
than others normally see.
I am shocked at the rage
I am capable of.
I fume at others—and occasionally at You—
and then hate myself for hating those I love.
I have been angry at those I hold dear,
and nurtured hurts caused by loved ones.

I ask Your blessing on my human frailty.
Heal my wounds, lest they fester.
I ask You for a love that is stronger than hurt,
that I may love the very ones
who have caused me pain.

For it is in pardoning that we rise above animals.
It is in forgiving we find our human nature.
A forgiving and healing love shows us who we are—
vessels of clay holding divine power and fragrance.

Make me more deeply human,
and draw me closer to You,
that I may know the joy of forgiving from my heart.

Remembering the Poor

With a sense of unworthiness,
with trepidation,
I think of the poor.

On any given day,
the world I call modern
sees more starvation and want
than prosperity and plenty.
I tend to forget this—
or to hide it behind respectable clichés.

The poor are uninteresting,
and I prefer to think, even in prayer,
of my small comfortable worries.
The poor remind me
that I have incredibly more than I need,
and I usually resent such reminders.

I prefer to deal with nameless statistics
and a faceless mankind.
I would rather not face
the desperate plight of real people—
hungry children, unemployed fathers, anemic
    mothers,
the homeless in our cities, the landless on our land,
the refugees without status, the little people without
    power.

The truth is frightening;
I feel helpless and angry.
Why do I have to look at this?
Why can't I enjoy my privileges in peace?
Why don't You let me live in happy indifference?
Why not let me pretend that my rights and desires
matter more than those of others?

I'd rather forget the ugly statistics
on man-made starvation and manipulated markets.
Don't remind me of men and women—
whom I mercifully seldom see—
working for a pittance
to provide me with comforts I have become used to.

Maybe, in all honesty,
I have no right to pray for the poor.
Maybe all I deserve is to pray for their forgiveness.
Maybe they teach me the way to a better world.

If I had the generosity to share
that many poor people have,
there would perhaps be enough and more for all.
Maybe I am the poor person, after all—
poor despite my plenty,
poor in humanity, poor in love,
frightened to death of losing what I have gathered.

I am afraid of praying for a better world.
I am afraid of having to share my plenty.
I'd rather say, "Isn't it awful!"
than do something to make it less awful.

Give me the courage not to hide behind cynicism
or escape into clever theories
that cover up my cowardice.
Help me to see other men and women
as human beings

with the same dreams and hopes as I.
Help me to build a human family in my own setting,
and not to close my heart to the cries of the
    powerless.

Let me not consider myself better or superior
because of what I have,
or despise neighbors or nations
because they possess less.

Teach us to reverence humanity—
Your divine presence within us—
even when appearances put us off.

May I never stoop
to measuring human worth
by what can be bought or measured.
Let me learn to see what I would be worth
if I were to lose the things I call my wealth.

Help me in my poverty!
Make me human,
richly and warmly human.

Open my eyes
that I may see the truth:
Our real wealth
is our humanity.
The measure of our greatness is our eagerness
to save what is left of it before it is too late—
before our hearts go bankrupt,
and we choke on selfishness and fear.

This greatness I crave for;
for this wisdom I pray.

For Those Who Suffer
More than I Do

Let me take into my heart
those who suffer more than I do—
those whose pains and needs are greater than mine.
Let me make room—a large inner space—
and take in the pains of the sick and the lonely,
the desperate and the dying.

Give me a heart
as large as the world's sorrows,
and a mind open to the weak and the powerless.

May I never become so absorbed in my own little
    world
as to forget my great human family.
May I see the world and all the suffering in it
with Your compassionate eyes,
with hope and courage,
with love and generosity,
with a sincere desire to help.

Let me never close my heart to the cry of the poor,
the pain of the oppressed,
and the agony of powerless victims.

I will not add to the world's load of hatred and pain;
I want to be a channel of healing and compassion.
Help me not to be so homebound as to forget
    mankind,
or so vaguely humanitarian

as to neglect those next to me.
Help me to remember
that, however thorny my problems,
there are always those who suffer more than I do.
However weak I may feel,
I am strong enough to bring comfort
to a brother or sister in greater need.

May I use my short life,
not to lament my lot
or the state of the world,
but to reach out in love
to those who suffer more than I do.

Help me to start right now.

For a Heart as Large as the World

You invite me in these quiet moments
to open my heart to all Your children.
These special moments spent with You
change me, not You.

I want to be more like You,
and make the world's longings my own.
I want to reach out in love to men, women and
    children
all over the world,
on every continent,
in every country, city and village—
people I understand and those I do not,
groups I feel close to,
and families "different" from mine.

I call down blessings
on all peoples and governments,
on those I consider friendly
and those I am taught to suspect;
on those I think of more often,
and others I seldom hear about.

Teach me to love all Your children,
and never hate or despise anyone You love.
Teach me to see the world as You see it—
as families and lonely hearts,
parents and children,

friends and lovers,
just like me and those I love.

Give me a courageous and effective love
that translates its good will into action.
Save me from polite indifference and fanatic hatred,
and from prejudice that blinds me
to what is new or different.

May we learn to see others
as human beings like ourselves,
and never allow the powerful
to maneuver us towards hatred.

Help us to come closer together as Your great family,
united in love, but not uniform in our ways.
May we overcome the barriers of suspicion and
   injustice,
and learn to treat others
as we want to be treated.

For Our Family

I bring to You our little family
with all our hopes and dreams.

You know what we need better than we do.
You love us far more than we can love each other.

Each one of us is a gift of Your love,
a gift to our family, a gift to the world.

Of all the wondrous ways in which You speak to me,
the first and the deepest,
the happiest and the hardest,
is the voice of my family.
I would not be what I am today
except for my dear ones.

Thank You for my family.
Thank You for everything we share.
Thank You for joy and laughter and tears and work,
and for the unique gifts each of us brings.
Thank You, above all, for the gift of love
which makes this our home—
a love we breathed and touched and knew
before we ever heard the word.
Thank You for this opportunity
to celebrate Your love for us.

Pardon us and heal us,
for we hurt each other.
Forgive us our lack of love,

our selfish withdrawal,
and words, deeds and silences that wound the heart.
We need Your healing everyday, every hour, every
moment.
Without Your constant care,
how could we hold each other in love?

Source of all love, make us aglow with love.
Make us thoughtful and caring,
generous in forgiving,
joyful in service,
open to give and to receive.

May our love and unity
open our hearts to You,
and to the great human family to which we belong.

May all families everywhere
know true love, peace and security.
May every family be a powerhouse of love,
a source of healing,
a place of joy.

And may we treat one another,
always and everywhere,
as members of Your one great family.

When I Don't Feel Like Praying

I am in no mood for prayer,
and I find myself talking about it.
When I have no taste for food,
I know that something is wrong.
When I have no taste for prayer,
well, what is that supposed to mean?

Why do I come to You?
Out of habit,
out of need,
and perhaps for reasons I do not know.

I remind myself
that Your first love
is not prayer, but our good.
We are the center of Your concern,
the reason for religion and worship,
these weak human beings You have chosen to love.

Shall I leave prayer for a while,
and talk about me?
Am I important enough for Your attention?
Or, will You listen to me
only if I follow the rules?
Do You love only pious people,
men and women who pray and talk to You?
Do we need to feel devout
before we have a word with You?

Tell me Your answers;
let us see if we think alike.

My questions somehow answer themselves.
The changing moods are mine, not Yours.
I measure love in thimbles, not You.
I wait to be asked before I help.
My affection has to be won;
it is not limitless, like Yours.

How do I talk to someone
who is so different from me?
You are all love, all wisdom, all power, they say.
You do not need my words, or my reminders.
You know me better than I know myself.

Help me to find meaning and the answers I need.
Teach me true worship.
Show me who I am.

Show me what love is,
and why I ought to pray.
Tell me what to do with my numberless questions.
Are You really as we imagine You?
You are not?
Then, who are You, and how do we find You?

I like to think of You as being on my side.
I want Your help to become better and happier.
If prayer and faith are about these matters,
then teach me, Lord—
teach me how to pray.

For the Gift of Humor

Give me something of Your divine humor—
that I may walk through life
with a light and easy step.
I am, after all, a child in Your house,
dealing with other, equally frightened, children.

Save me from pompous conceit,
from the desire to act as wisdom incarnate,
from the dreariness that parades as duty,
and from dull rigidity that wears the mask of virtue.

Help me to admit, and laugh at,
my inevitable mistakes.
(If I see ten,
there must be a hundred I do not see.)
Give me eyes to enjoy
the numberless occasions for laughter—
but never in scorn or the desire to hurt.
May I not confuse seriousness with solemnity,
devotion with dryness, detachment with coldness.
May I not be so absorbed in my big little problems
that I have no eyes for the pranks of children,
or for the comic situations
in which we see ourselves for the children we are.

May my chats with You be free of rigidity and pomp.
Save me from the weight of self-righteous ideas,
and from a piety that puts people off.

May I never become a pious bore or a religious
    fanatic,
a self-proclaimed messiah
with all the right answers!
May I never take myself too seriously,
or end up worshiping my ideas about You.
Forgive me the foolishness that oozes from my clever
words.
Let us laugh at them together, You and I.

In our great laughter,
with moist eyes and a carefree heart,
I'll see the one great truth—
that You alone matter,
You and Your unspeakable love for us,
Your love that is full of patience and humor.

All the rest is vanity, vanity of vanities.
How foolish we are to take it all so seriously!
But You won't punish us for being foolish, will You?
You are God, after all, full of tenderness and humor,
and You cannot bear hurting Your children,
even when we act as if we were more than human.
                    HA! HA! HA!

In Old Age

There is no need of niceties before You,
and I can just be myself.
I hate admitting it,
I dread saying it aloud:
I am old,
I feel old, and
I don't like it too much.

How I miss health and youth and movement,
and the incredible freedom to do what I wanted!
I have to face the truth
that I will not be young again,
that many doors are closed for good.
I feel embarrassed to be dependent;
it hurts to be considered old—and old-fashioned.

At times I wonder:
Am I being a burden?
Are the remaining years empty, without meaning?

In my confusion and solitude,
You stretch out Your hand,
the hand that never left me all these years.
You whisper to me secrets I did not know before.
You tell me that every season has its own beauty,
that a year is not made only of summer.

There are strengths my age gives me,
gifts which others need—

compassion and tolerance,
wisdom and humor,
and the wonderful opportunity
to let others move up.

I have had my place at life's banquet;
let me gracefully watch someone else take my place.
It is good for me to step aside
and enjoy the sunset,
as others take over tasks I once fulfilled.

May they learn from my serenity that aging is a
  grace.
May my failings teach them caution and balance.
There is so much more to life
than work and movement;
we grow also in stillness and in letting go.

I thank You
for these years of leisure,
for the dear ones who give me their time and their
  love,
for my memory, my health and the powers I still
  have.

Thank You for the beauty of nature,
the laughter of children,
and all the signs of life around us.
Thank You for books and music
and what the media provide.

Thank You, above all,
for the assurance of Your presence,
for the strength You give me each new day.
Thank You for the serenity I frequently experience,
and for the limitations that teach me to let go.

Help me in my weariness.
Strengthen me in my weakness.

Fill my solitude with the warmth of Your presence.
Hold my hand when I falter;
be with me now more than ever,
and prepare me for my final journey.

For I know
this is only the beginning, not the end.
This life I cherish is but a shadow
of what awaits me after death.
This world I cling to is not my true home.
Increase my faith and my hope,
that I may feel Your touch
all through the day and the night.
Transform my vision,
that I may see the feast to which You call me.

Help me never to forget
that, even when I cannot pray or think of You,
I am never lost to Your sight.
All the good things I have received from Your hands
teach me to trust You completely,
to entrust myself totally to You.
I do so now, with all my heart,
and ask for Your strength and Your protection.

Continue to be with me,
and keep me in Your heart—
in a warm little corner reserved all for me.
This is all I need;
this is all I ask.

Facing My Death

Teach me to let go.

You understand better than I do
my fantasies, my fears, my clinging,
my desire to hold on to this one life that I know.

I believe
that you will call me
when it is best for me.
I believe
that Your love has prepared for me
joys beyond my grasp.
I know
that You forgive all my faults.

And yet,
like a child clinging to its broken but familiar toys,
I am reluctant to let go.
I am frightened of the unknown and the unfamiliar.
I see only darkness
where You promise me light.
I see only the end of life
where true life begins for me.

You understand my human clinging,
and my sense of incompleteness.
It is You who made and fashioned me,
and gave me feelings and fantasies.
You see my need to be held, to be led,
to be taken over paths I do not know.

My strength fails,
my cleverness is of no avail;
my loved ones cannot come with me.
You alone—
my one unfailing love on life's solitary journey—
You will be there at my side,
as You have always been.
You will hold me,
guide me,
receive me,
and remake my broken frame.

Before You, I have no secrets.
I do not hide my fears, or my lack of answers.
It is all right, strangely,
to be weak and powerless and afraid.
I need not deny anything.
I want to be remade.
I want to fall asleep in Your arms
and awake in eternal light.

I do not see or understand.
But I believe, my God,
my infinite and tender God,
that love can do everything—
that eye has not seen,
ear has not heard,
what You have prepared for me after death.

In Your name, I surrender
the remaining hours or years of my life,
knowing that the best is yet to come.

Here I come!
Be with me all through my last journey,
and take me home to be with You forever.

I Want to Be Free!

Thank You for this desire for freedom,
which is itself Your gift.
Teach me the true meaning of freedom,
and help me to become free.

Show me the numberless ways I keep myself bound,
and break the chains of my slavery.
I am a slave to more tyrants than one—
fear and greed and crippling habits,
and wallowing in weakness
when I can be strong.

I see slavery in me and around me—
chains that bind me,
chains that bind mankind,
structures and ways that are rooted in sin.
Show me true freedom,
and help me to liberate my world.
Help me to break free
of the habit of indifference,
cowardice in its many forms,
and prejudice that blinds me.

Free me from the tyranny of my past,
and from a vision that ignores Your work among us.
Free me from habits that weigh me down,
from opinions that shackle my thought,
and from attachments which form a prison.
May I be a channel of hope and liberation,

free and freeing, as Your love always is.
May we work together to conquer
ignorance and prejudice,
cowardice and oppression,
and all that keeps us from being Your family.
May we never reduce freedom to narrow self-interest,
nor claim it as a right only for ourselves.
Teach us what it means to be truly free—
free from without and free from within.
Free us incessantly from a slavish outlook,
and from a desire to make slaves of others.

Make us free!
Teach us to be free and to work for freedom—
to suffer and die for it, if the need arose.
May we freely choose what is noblest and best,
and thus come to know the freedom of Your children.

As Your children,
we will do the good You ask us to do,
and do it cheerfully and with supreme freedom.
We will work for a world
where we promote—never destroy—
each other's sacred right to grow in freedom.

If Only I Had Faith!

I reach out into the darkness
where You love to hide,
and grope for signs of Your presence.

Are You there?
Are You really there?
Am I deceiving myself
when I trust You, talk to You,
and try to live by what I think You want?

At times I wish
I were surer of Your presence.
I wish I could touch You,
see You, hear You, feel You . . .
At other times
I forget You almost entirely,
and go ahead as if You did not exist.

But You send out feelers seeking my response.
You move me, disturb me,
almost convince me without proofs.

Who needs proofs anyway?
They are useless to the one who believes,
and a laughing matter for those who do not.
What I want is faith—
a rock to lean on,
a love to respond to,
an answer to my numberless questions,

warmth and light I need,
and a passion to keep me moving.

Am I a believer? Perhaps not yet.
Am I an unbeliever? Perhaps not fully.
Do these categories matter? Probably no, to You.

But all I have
are my human words and my human search,
words and questions from my short and confused
    journey.
I do not know how to address You.
I dare not think I have found the answers.
I am not even sure I'm asking the right questions.
And I have only this short and groping life
for thinking and searching and believing.

And so,
from the bottom of my dark little well,
I cry to You for faith—
for a vision to give me meaning,
for a guiding hand to direct my steps,
for a home where I truly belong.
I bring to You my doubts, my questions,
my answers, the numerous opinions I have heard,
the conflicting claims to allegiance
and, above all, my silence.

May I find You in my silence;
may my words never drown Your voice.
Both my words and my silence are a quest for You.
You wait for me in the working of my mind
and in its resting.

You have drawn me out of myself
and set my feet in Your direction.
I'll rest only when I find You,
my source, my end,

my God without name or face.
Keep me open to finding You
where I may least expect to find You.

Ah, yes!—I see it now, I begin to see it—
You have been with me all the while,
and I was chasing a fantasy of what You should be
   like.
I ask no more.
I need no words.
You are here, in this passing moment,
and I need not look for You.

It was I who was far away,
and You came in search of me.
Let me take Your hand and stay where I belong.
Lead me where I am meant to go.
Show me what I long to see.

When Joy Fills My Heart

I feel so happy today, so happy, so happy!
I am bursting with joy!
I feel alive!
I'm all that I want to be.

Tears fill my eyes.
Speechless for joy,
I feel aglow with warmth.
I could scream like a child!
Oh, yes, I could!

These moments of ecstasy
make everything so light, so easy.
How good You are to me!
How beautiful life is!
How wonderful it is to be alive!

How I'd love to feel this way forever,
and fill every passing moment
from the overflow of this instant.

Thank You for the gift of joy!
Thank You for making me capable of ecstasy!
Thank You for the happiness
that heals me and makes me whole.
Thank You for this foretaste of heaven.

In silent wonder,
I'll stand before You
and let the torrents of Your love

bathe me and soften me.
I will let joy break through my defenses,
and show me the silent Giver who gives without
    measure.

O my Love, my Joy, my Unending Happiness,
thank You for the radiance of this moment!
Thank You for breaking down the timid walls of my
    heart
with the gentle showers of Your joy!
Thank You for making me too great for this world
and too precious to be forgotten by You.

You are greater than my heart,
and this joy I feel is but a small sign of Your touch.
Touch me again,
and send me out into Your world
as a sign and bearer of Your joy!

At One's Wits' End

Where do I turn for help?
What do I tell You?

I don't even know where to start.
I have a trillion things on my mind,
and every one of them seems urgent.
I feel lost, confused; I'm frightened.
I am like a dry leaf blown about in the storm,
without energy, without purpose,
carried away to who knows where!

Hurry up, and save me!
My feet are sinking in the mire.
I have no energy left.

Come to my rescue!
Save me!
Stretch out Your mighty hand,
and pull me out of the pit of despair.

You are my one hope,
my refuge,
the only one I can turn to.

Do not wait any longer,
for without Your help I am lost.
I feel so frightened, so lonely, so confused.

Please listen!
Make haste and come down!
Do You not see? I need You!

I need You so much.
I need You right now.
Help me!
Please, help me!

When Prayers Seem Unanswered

What's the use of talking to You
if You don't seem to listen?
I was told: "Ask, and you shall receive."
I asked—and received nothing.
Nothing but disappointment!

Why should I talk to You again?
Does it make any difference
whether we talk to You,
or ignore You altogether?
Do You care about what happens to us?
Does it hurt You to see us hurt,
or are You so distant
that we do not matter to You?

Am I asking for the wrong things?
Is that why You refuse them?
Or, am I not ready yet
to be flooded with Your blessings?
What are You telling me through Your silence?

I will knock again, and ask, and insist.
I am Your child, and You *have* to listen.
If You don't listen,
to whom shall I go?
Is there anyone who loves me more than You do?

If You love me so much,
why do You not listen?
Show me how to ask, and what to ask for.

If my heart is set on harmful ways,
correct me.
If I seek foolish, dangerous gifts,
do not grant them.

But if what I ask is for my good,
please hear me!
Hear me now!
Grant my prayer!

I am tired of waiting, waiting so long!
Are You deaf?
Are You blind?
Do You not care?
If You care, then show it!

Save me, give an answer.
Hear my prayer!
Grant my request!

I will knock, I will ask, I will insist,
till You open the door and reach out to me.

Thank You!

There is so much I owe You,
I do not know where to begin.

Your favors are numberless; who can count them?
Thank You that I am alive and able to say thanks.
Thank You for all that I have, all that I am.

You do not expect any thanks, You say?
Oh, thank You, then, for that—
for loving me without conditions,
without waiting to be thanked.

This is beyond my poor human grasp—
that love can be so complete as to give all,
and give all without asking anything in return.

What shall I tell You,
how can I thank You?
Anything I say is apt,
as long as it comes from my heart.
You do not want sacrifices, flattery,
clever words, or compliments.
There is nothing we can give You,
no way we can pay You back.

You, whose name is love,
rejoice at our joys.
You delight in doing us good.
You wait close by, eager to do us good.

You make the sun shine on the grateful
and on the ungrateful.

When we feel inspired to praise You,
it is not to bribe You
with our foolish and well-meant words of praise,
but to draw even more fully
from the wells of Your tenderness.

Thank You for such unspeakable love!
I have not even begun to understand
what You have done for me,
what You will do for me,
or what Your love is capable of doing.

Thank You! Thank You! Thank You!
Accept my words, my helpless silence,
my whole being in thanksgiving!

Is this all You ask of me:
that I be as happy as I can be,
and let Your love flood my heart
and flow through me?

Is this Your dream for me:
to make me—
stubborn, unseeing me—
as totally loving as You are?
This, then, I want—
only teach my frightened heart to let go.

Oh, what joy to think that, right now, at this instant,
Your loving gaze is turned toward me,
that You hold me tenderly in Your arms,
that You only wait for me to let You love me!

Thank You, my God, my Love, my Everything!
Thank You for this desire to thank You!

Too Tired to Think or to Pray

I feel so tired, as You can see;
I'm in no mood for deep thoughts and prayers.

Thank You for my health and chances to be active.
I offer You all that I have done,
and the fatigue I feel in every limb.

Let me relax in Your loving arms,
and entrust all my cares to You!

Refresh me with rest.
Give me new life by Your power.
Help me to accept my limitations,
and to receive fresh strength from You.

You are my strength, my solace,
my fountain of life-giving water.

I sit, I lie down to rest;
I rest in You.
I surrender;
I let go;
I let You take over.

I Know—I Do Not Know

As I light the little candle of my knowledge,
I notice a few things in the dim light.
I look at them, and try to see beyond them.
I am curious, I am fascinated; I feel lost in wonder.

For every grain of knowledge I have gathered,
there is a whole seashore of unexplored beauty.
I am like a child turning over in my hand
the little pebble I have picked up.
The mountainside is too much for me,
the oceans are beyond my grasp;
this little handful I call knowledge
is all I can handle.

I do not know why I am alive,
or when I will die.
I do not see how these marks on paper
become ideas and change me.
I was not there when the world began,
nor do I grasp the mystery of time.
This moment—no, it is gone! I cannot stop it.

I know that I do not know
who You are and how You love us.
I hardly understand what makes grass green,
or how mud and sunshine design roses.
I do not even know
how many thoughts there are in my head,

or how deeply I can love.
Galaxies and fingertips are both mysterious gifts.

Playful Lover,
why did You give me a mind with endless questions?
Why did You hide treasures for me to discover?
I do not know.
Even when I say I know,
what I really mean is:
I trust those who say they know.
But do they know?

We constantly push back the tide of ignorance,
and claim a little more land we call knowledge.
And just when we begin to congratulate ourselves,
we notice new oceans, new horizons, more distant
    stars.
Under Your watchful guidance,
we explore our world and its mysteries,
and we feel proud of what we have found out.
You rejoice at our little steps
and lovingly show us
another stretch of Your garden of surprises.

We begin to see that all we have discovered
is only a beginning, a wonderful beginning.
Our greatest discovery
is our own endlessness,
for we are arrows shot into the infinite.
The journey never ends;
the newness never fades;
the heart never grows old.

I know that I do not know.
I know that You know.
You knew it all the while,
and You drew me on with the thirst to know.

As I reach for the stars,
may I look into my heart,
and see the gentle radiance that keeps me searching.

I do not know what I will find,
or even what I really seek.
What I do know
is that small answers are not enough for me.

I want everything.
I want light.
I want You.

Special Persons

Thinking of Someone I Love

In the morning fill me with Your love;
I will exult and rejoice all my days.

I rejoice in this passing moment
in which Your love waits for me.

Thank You for Your love,
and for the people who make it real for me.
I thank You especially for ————'s love for me
and my love for ————.

Thank You for all the beauty in me and around me,
and for the wonderful way You have made me.

All through this day
may Your word be a lamp for my steps;
may Your love be the source of my strength;
may Your arms protect me from all harm.

May I see You and love You in everyone I meet today,
and seek the truth with all the passion of my heart.
I ask the same grace for all those I love,
and for the whole world.

In You I trust;
to You I belong.
Guard me and those I love as the apple of Your eye.

A Mother's Prayer

Thank You for the privilege of being a mother.

Thank You for this undeserved grace—
to share Your love with my children,
to give life, and to nurture it with my care,
to bring up my children on the right path,
and to be the privileged channel of Your love for
   them.

Thank You for the trust You have placed in me—
for entrusting to my care
sons and daughters who are more precious
than all the marvels of this world.

Thank You for my family,
and for all those who support us with their love.
Thank You for the countless gifts we receive every
   day,
especially for the power to love, to forgive, and to
   care.

Forgive me for the times I fail.
Pardon my weakness, my ingratitude, and my sins.

Help me to remember
that You never lose sight of me;
that You watch over my dear ones
with unspeakable tenderness.

You are my Creator:
all that I am, all those I love, are your gift.
You are my Father, my Saviour, my Friend:
Your love will never forsake me.

In You I trust.
From You I accept my children.
To You I commend them and their future.

Keep us safe in the shelter of Your hand.
Guide us all to that Happy Home,
where there will be no more tears,
no more divisions,
and no shadow of evil—
a Home You have prepared for us
with a love far greater
than a mother's.

A Father's Prayer

I never knew,
I never imagined
how much fatherhood would change me.

Now I know a little more clearly
what tenderness You feel for me.
Thank You, Father, for trusting me so much,
for entrusting a family to my care.

Thank You for showing me
that I can be strong and tender,
strict and flexible,
demanding and so very vulnerable.
My children have changed me,
changed me for the better.
I do not deserve the gifts I see in them,
nor the joy each of them is to me.
They are Your gift, they and everything we have.

There is so much I long to do for them,
so many things I want to give them.
I want to be the best of fathers,
and give them the world!
You remind me, patiently and with love,
that the world is not enough for them.

True.

Help me, then, to give them all they need—
love and protection,

security and example,
and the serenity of a loving home united in Your love.

Teach me to discipline my children with love,
to correct them wisely,
and to be an example they will love to follow.

Protect my children from all harm, bodily and
   spiritual.
Help me to understand each of them in their
   uniqueness,
and to provide for their needs as best I can.
Teach me how to prod the hesitant, curb the rash
   ones,
and never quench their love of life.

Show me when to be strict, and when to be gentle,
how much to demand and what to overlook.
Grant that, in everything I do or pass over in silence,
I may affirm their worth, their beauty, and their gifts.

Help me to look beyond our home
to Your great human family,
with all its treasures and its many needs.

Forgive me my failures,
and the bad example I have given.
You know better than I do
how confused and helpless I can feel,
even when I look strong and confident.

Steady my hand and my heart
that, through everything I do or say,
my children may see Your wisdom
and feel Your fatherly care.

Father,
help me to be a true father!

For Mother and Father

I bless You for my parents,
and I ask Your blessing on them.

I do not understand them as they deserve,
nor do they always know what I really want.
But I know this—
they have done for me
more than I realize;
the price they have paid is higher than I see.

I expect perfection,
forgetting they are human,
and I want my parents to meet all my demands.
How can they?

Thank You, dear Lord,
for my father and mother.
Thank You for all that they have given me—
their time, their youth, their health, their possessions,
and, above all, themselves in love.

Help me to love them as I ought,
and to give them what they need.
Help me to understand them
in their greatness and their limitations,
and never add to their burdens.
Help me to forgive their inevitable mistakes,
and to keep only the good they have taught me.

Give my parents, and all parents everywhere,
courage and hope in their task,
joy in their children,
and possibilities to realize their dreams.

I shall never be able to repay
what my parents have done for me.
I entrust them, now and always,
to Your love—
a love far greater than all we know.

Your love reached me first through my parents.
May it now reach them through me,
and bring them joy, strength and comfort.

May we never destroy the circle of caring
in which Your tender wisdom has placed us.
May we grow in You everyday
and show Your goodness to one another.

A Couple's Prayer

We join our hands and our hearts today,
as we come for Your blessing.
Touch our hearts,
and lead us closer to You and to each other.

Heal us of all that divides us.
Take away all that keeps us
from the fullness of love You dream for us.

We have been blessed with the gift of each other,
and in this union
we have experienced
Your presence and Your healing.

We have known the thrill of love,
the soothing balm of pardon,
the pain of rejection,
the anguish of broken promises.

You have walked with us every step of the way,
and invited us to go on when we were tired.
You gave us strength for the journey
and fresh energy and warmth when our hearts grew
    cold.
You have been patient with our failures,
and You invite us to be patient with ourselves
and with our partner.

By coming together,
we tasted something of Your love

and Your unfailing fidelity.
We learned to read the book of life
with each other's eyes,
seeing what we could not have seen alone.

We have enriched each other;
we have disappointed each other.
We need renewal and healing—
constant renewal and incessant healing.
We need to draw from a reservoir of love
that is never empty—You.

Fill our hearts with Your love
that we may cherish each other till we die.
Heal us of fear and selfish pursuits,
that we may surrender ourselves in joy.

May You be the source of our love.
May our love renew us every day.
May it overflow into tender concern
for all those You send into our lives—
our family and friends, our neighbors and loved ones,
and all those we will meet today.

Thank You for the gift of each other.
Thank You for Your love.
Thank You for the healing and the hope
You bring us each new day.

A Teenager's Prayer

Are You my friend,
a real friend I can count on?
A true, honest friend who will stand by me,
and not be put off by my acting out?

If so,
I want to talk to You today—
about myself, my world, my friends,
the endless questions I have,
the hundred and one things we talk about,
and the things I never tell anyone.

Will You find me boring?
(I find You boring at times—
especially when they make You sound
like a stern, stuffy boss,
waiting to catch me when I do wrong.)

Do You like me?
Do my chats really interest You?
Do I have a place in Your heart? In Your plans?
I know I feel Your touch at special moments—
but I feel shy to talk about it.
There are times when I feel called
to a generous life of courage,
a life of service—
but soon, a hundred other attractions crowd it out.

I am pulled in so many directions;
I feel like a bundle of contradictions.

I feel like a child at times—
but want to be treated like a grown-up.
I fear being treated like a grown-up,
and want to be looked after,
almost like a child.

I want to be reassured I am likable,
that I'll succeed,
that the changing moods are OK.
I want to be sure that I count,
that my life is worth living.

I do not have proper words to talk to You.
But You can see my sincerity and my good will,
and You understand me better than anyone else.
You know everything about me,
and still You love me totally.
You understand my most hidden secrets,
and do not laugh at what I think or say.

Be my friend always, and help me to believe in
    myself,
and in life.
Help me to learn from others' mistakes and from my
    own—
and to admit my failures.
Do not let me waste my youth in selfish and idle
    pursuits.
Teach me rather to use these years
to learn who I am, and what I want.

Under Your loving gaze,
I will treat myself with patience and respect,
and really grow up, not just grow old.

May I be a better person than I was yesterday,
and may the world be a better place because of me.

A Teacher's Prayer

Give me, Divine Master,
a sincere love for my students,
and deep respect for each one's unique gifts.
Help me to be a faithful and devoted teacher,
with my eyes on the good of those I serve.

May I impart knowledge humbly,
listen attentively,
collaborate willingly,
and seek the lasting good of those I teach.

May I be quick to understand,
slow to condemn,
eager to affirm and to forgive.

While I teach ideas and give training in skills,
may my life and my integrity
open minds and hearts to the truth.
May my warmhearted interest in each one
give them a zest for life and a passion for learning.
Give me the strength to admit my limitations,
the courage to start each day with hope,
and the patience and humor I need in my teaching.

I accept each student from Your hands.
I believe that every one of them
is a person of unique worth,
even when they themselves do not see it.
I know that I have the opportunity

to bring light and hope,
a sense of mission and purpose
to many young lives.
I believe that You believe in me,
and You stand by me.

I seek Your blessing
as I start another day.
I ask You to bless me and my students,
and our dreams and hopes.

May we learn from the wisdom of the past.
May we learn from life and from one another.
May we, above all,
learn from Your guidance
and from the lives of those who know You best.

For this is true learning:
to know life as it should be lived;
to know ourselves as we truly are,
and to hear Your voice in every word we learn.

A Student's Prayer

The more I learn,
the better I see how little I know—
and how little I know of my own capacity to know.
I see that each branch of knowledge
is so rich, so complex,
one can study a lifetime
and still be a beginner.

Teach me how to learn wisely and well.
Help me to master the subjects I need to study,
and never give in to despair or boredom.
Help me to remember how fortunate I am
to be able to study, to grow in knowledge.
Give me wisdom,
that I may treasure knowledge,
and never forget how little I know.

Help me to be diligent, without undue ambition,
and successful, without worshiping success.
Teach me to give each task
its rightful place,
and use my talents to the best of my ability.

Make me strong against temptations,
resolute before distractions,
humble before the truth, and
gracious to the less gifted.

Give me a vision larger than my studies
and greater than my individual success.
Teach me to use my opportunities gratefully,
develop my talents responsibly,
and place my learning
at the service of truth and justice.

May I keep learning all through my life,
knowing that, however much I may learn,
there are always new worlds to discover.

Make me wise and strong,
that I may learn from life itself,
consider everyone as my teacher,
and never turn away from the light of Your face.

Special Occasions

Before the Birth of a Child

Thank You for blessing us so richly,
for sharing with us Your own power to give life.

This is a mystery we will never fathom,
a marvel far beyond all human understanding.
Thank You for bringing us together in love.
Thank You for all that we enjoy in each other.
Thank You, above all, for this new life.

We are left speechless, we feel such a sense of awe,
as we accept this sign of Your trust—
this new life,
the fruit of our bodies,
the fruit of our love,
the mysterious reminder
that we are more than ourselves.
Thank You, Creator and Lord,
our Father, our Mother, our infinitely loving God!

We accept this new life from Your bounty.
We promise to guard it, treasure it,
be worthy of Your trust.
We'll look into our hearts and make them new,
so as to be the best of parents.

Increase our love, that we may reflect Your love.
Give us health of body and mind,
and shelter us from all harm,

that we may give our child
all the tender care it needs.

May this period of waiting
be free of all dangers,
untroubled by anguish
and full of peace and good health.

Help us to prepare our hearts and our home
for our child.
Bless us with Your protection.
We pray for health, safety,
and freedom from all dangers,
for the three of us
and for all expectant mothers and fathers.
Bless us with a peaceful confinement,
a safe delivery
and the priceless grace of holding
a normal, healthy baby in our arms.

May Your grace and our love
accompany our child always,
every moment,
from now till eternity.

On My Birthday

Thank You, Father,
for the gift of life,
for this undeserved grace I receive constantly.
Thank You for this marvelous secret,
this most precious of gifts which I take for granted.
You call me into being
every passing instant,
and I would not exist, except by Your grace.

Thank You for thinking of me,
creating me,
placing me in Your great world
in the company of good and loving people.
Thank You for my parents, my family,
and all those who have loved me
and taught me how to love.

Bless all those who have cared
for my health and well-being,
all those who have helped me to love life.
Bless everyone who remembers me on this birthday.
Thank You
for the unique gifts You have given me,
for my health and strength, senses and memory,
for the power to think, to love and to understand.

Thank You for the year of life I have had
and for the years or moments
that You will still give me on this earth.

All the beauty I have seen,
all the love I have received and given,
all the things I have been able to do,
were Your gifts—
gifts that came to me unasked,
undeserved,
totally without pay.

What more has Your love prepared for me?
What marvels of Your tender mercy
are still hidden from my sight?

You invite me to trust You in the future,
and to expect still greater gifts from You.
I will look forward, then,
to the time that still remains,
with hope, with excitement, with peace.

My birthdays remind me
of the greatness of Your love,
the goodness of my dear ones,
and the fleeting pace of life.

As I enjoy this life and the love I give and receive,
prepare my heart for my Great Birthday,
when You will welcome me to my true and endless
   life,
with gifts far beyond my wildest fantasies.

May that birthday be the best of all.

Visiting a Sick Person

I bring before You
———, whom we love.
May my love and the love of many others
give her strength.
Heal her and bring her back to us.

We believe that You never leave us.
In Your loving arms we are forever secure.
Both health and sickness are blessings,
each teaching us to treasure life and love.

Bless ——— in her illness.
Make her aware of Your loving presence.
Hold her tenderly in Your arms;
give her peace,
and speak to her heart.
Give her the grace
to grow through this illness.

Watch over ——— in her aloneness
Shelter her from all harm.
Heal her and give her back to us.
Heal her soon, for we want to celebrate Your mercy.

May this illness, and our concern for one another,
help us grow in love, in faith and in wisdom.
May it bring us closer to one another and to You.

Written for a sick woman. The "she" and "her" have to be changed, of course, while praying for a man.

May we see Your love in all that befalls us,
and respond to You with trusting surrender.

Be with ———
and with each one of us.
Give us health;
give us serenity;
fill us with Your peace.

At a Celebration

We thank You
for this day of joy—
for the memories we share,
for the friends we meet today;
for the health You give us
to enjoy their presence and Your gifts.

May this celebration give us
a taste of Your love.
May it bind us closer together,
and make us grateful for the numberless gifts
we receive everyday.

Thank You for bringing us to this day.
Thank You for the loved ones
whose presence makes us happy,
and for the absent ones
who are with us in spirit.

We pray for all those who have toiled with love
to make this a happy day,
especially ———— and ————

We are gathered in Your name.
We will stay together in joy,
and go forth with grateful hearts.

Nearby or far away,
may we support one another
with a genuine and lasting love.

At Work

Thank You for work—
for our capacity to think and plan, dream and act;
for our ability to make things and improve our lot.

This paper, this print, this room,
the clothes I wear, the food I eat,
the medicines that help me, the house I live in—
all this I owe to work.

Thank You for making us makers of our history.
Thank You for sharing Your creative energies with us.
Thank You for my healthy mind and body,
through which I can understand and fashion my
    world.

Bless my work
and all those I work with.
Help us to work together in harmony and justice.
May we put the welfare of people
at the heart of our planning,
and use our skills to build a better world.

May we not seek profit at the expense of others,
nor use our gifts to rob the defenseless.
Help us to work diligently,
but without anxiety;
and learn to do better,
without hurting others.

Help us to treat each other with genuine respect,
and to seek solutions that are fair and honest.
May we contribute our share
with dignity and diligence,
and make the world of work
a meeting of equals.
May we unfold Your marvels
through our creativity,
and imitate Your largesse
towards those who have less.

While we work and provide for ourselves,
may we not forget
that there is more to life than work,
and far more to work than just being busy.

Through our activity
lead us to the fullness we silently seek.
Help us to remember that we are worth
infinitely more than the work of our hands.
You have made us for a goal far greater than work—
to see You, love You, love ourselves in You,
and to share Your love with everyone we meet.

May we move to this goal in everything we do;
may all our work flow from a quiet and loving heart.

On My Day Off

I looked forward to this day of rest.
What a blessing it is to sit and think,
be with my dear ones and be refreshed in spirit.

This pause helps me to become more human,
and to look at the things that really matter—
life and love, the passing of time,
the goodness of people, the beauty of nature.
Numberless are the ways in which You speak to us.
You wait for us to be quiet,
and to notice Your love behind Your gifts,
so that we may find fresh hope
and strength for our journey.

Thank You for this moment of quiet.
Thank You for reminding me
that I count more than the work I do.
The people I meet, the loved ones I call mine,
need *me*—not just my work.
I often forget that the best gift I can give them
is to become more loving, more human, more alive.

I invite You into my heart
in this hour of silence.
Help me to relax in Your gentle presence.
Give me new life, new hope, new strength.

Show me what I fail to see in the thick of daily
    battles.
Make me human, more deeply human.

Thank You for all Your priceless gifts—
my family, my friends, all the love in my life;
the beauty of things, sounds, sights and color.
Thank You for my health, my body, my mind,
my freedom to work, to move, to pause.
Thank You for life, this rich, colorful mosaic,
a gift I receive each moment anew.
Thank You for the serenity of this moment.
Thank You for Your presence, which never leaves me.

With a joyful heart
I celebrate Your gifts.
I celebrate life;
I celebrate grace.
I celebrate each moment
of my short earthly journey,
seeing that every single instant is a grace.

And right now, as I look into Your eyes,
my life sparkles in the glow of Your touch.

During Travel

I bless You
for the marvels of travel—
for the machines that bring us closer together,
and for the creative mind You have given us
to invent better and safer modes of travel.

I ask Your blessing on this journey,
on all my fellow passengers,
and on those in charge of our safety and comfort.
I recommend to You especially
those who are anxious or ill,
and those with urgent goals in mind.
Remember the loved ones we have left behind,
and the people we are going to meet.

May we enjoy the journey
and reach our destination
in safety and joy.

May our chances to travel farther and faster
bring us closer together as one human family.
May our journey through life open our hearts and
   minds
to Your creation and to You,

and bring us safely to the destination
we are meant to reach.

Guide and protect us
so that we may never lose our way,
or forget our goal.

At Death and Bereavement

Accept these tears as my prayer.
Watch with me, please, and give me strength!

I have no words to tell You what I feel.
You need no words to hear my cry.
Be with me, please, and hold my hand,
for I feel frightened and alone.

I knew, of course,
that death would part us one day.
But when the hour did come,
what a wrench it was!
A part of me died and was buried with ———.
I feel like a shadow of what I was before.

Receive my ——— into Your loving embrace.
Someone I loved much, but in my own poor way,
is certainly better off with You.
I could not give him/her
all that he/she yearned for;
You can.
Help me to accept this truth,
and to rejoice in it.

I believe—I try to tell myself—
that death is not the end, but a passage—
a passage to unspeakable glory and life without end.
But I—I cannot see that or grasp it.
I am only human; I am in pain and alone.

I can only see up to this door,
not the light that shines beyond it.

So, while I hope, while I trust, while I accept Your
 will,
strengthen my faith and give me courage.

I thank You for the love we have given each other.
I ask Your pardon for the hurts we have caused.
I accept all—life, death, eternity—
as undeserved gifts from Your mercy.

Throw Your arms around me,
and comfort me!
See my tears! Hear my cry!
Turn my pain into hope,
my loneliness into wisdom, and
my fear into new strength for the new day.

May this death teach me to prepare for my death,
and to pass my days in loving gratitude.
All that You do for us is love,
even when we do not understand it.
I do not seek to understand.
I ask for hope, for strength, for serenity.

Accept these tears; they are all I have now.
Bless me! Give me hope!
Out of my mourning,
bring new life for me and for those I love.

Every Day, Every Night

Thank You for This New Day

Thank You, Lord, for this new day.
Thank You for those who love me and care for me.
Thank You for the wonder of my being,
for gifts of mind, heart and body.
Thank You for all the good things I enjoy
and the trials which make me strong.

Help me
to make the best of every hour of this day.
Save me from fear, selfishness and greed.
Help me to enjoy the love I receive,
and to share my love with a glad and generous heart.

May no one suffer today because of me;
may no one go hungry because of my greed.
May no one be lonely because I do not care.
May my heart be open to those who need me.

May I grow today in strength, in joy, in love.
May I seek what is true, noble and pure.
May I begin and end this day in Your presence,
and walk through my life secure, for I'm never alone.

Thank You for Your love, Your presence, Your
    protection.
Thank You for guarding me as the apple of Your eye.

Composed for the International Youth Year (1985); set to music by Olympio D'Mello, S.D.B. The musical score is given in *Youth Worker's Resource Book* by Felix Koikara and Joe Mannath (Madras: Don Bosco Publications, 1985), p. 34.

An Evening Remembrance

I want to end this day in Your company.
There is much my heart wants to tell You.
You have been with me all through this day;
shall we go over our time together?

Thank You
for this day of life,
for all that it brought me—
the opportunities I was given,
the people I met,
the conversations I had,
the knowledge I gained,
the love I gave and received.

I look back upon the joys I experienced,
at the tasks I was able to complete,
at the satisfaction this day brought me.

I also look at my disappointments and failures,
at the jobs left unfinished,
at the pain I caused,
at the good I left undone,
at memories that still hurt.

Open my eyes to the wonders You worked today
in the world and in me.
Open my heart to accept
Your pardon and Your peace.

Teach me to end this day
in trustful surrender.

In You I trust.
To You I belong.
To Your love I entrust
all those who died today
and their dear ones who mourn;
and those who are on their deathbed right now.

No one is lost to Your sight;
may they also be present to my heart:
those who work all night;
all travelers
and those in charge of their safety;
all those who had a difficult day,
or fear the oncoming night;
those in pain,
and those who are too lonely to rest or to pray.

May these evening hours
prepare me for the great evening of my life,
when I will look back on life's day,
and find no words
to thank You
for all the love I will have received.

Teach Me How to Talk to You

Teach me
how to speak with You,
how to talk to You with faith and trust.

My mind is a crowded marketplace.
Unless I build a temple to You,
there is no corner where I can listen to love.

I enter my temple.
I wait.
I listen . . .

There are times when I sense Your presence,
and feel calm and secure in Your nearness.
There are days and weeks, however,
when You are far from my thoughts,
and prayer seems such a heavy, boring task,
an archaic ritual,
a tiresome repetition of words without meaning.

You remind me in my better moments
that I am dearer to You than places of worship,
that You only ask what is for my good.
Everything I undergo, every breath I take,
matters to You as though You had no other care.

May I have the wisdom to seek Your touch in quiet
    moments.
May I take time to be refreshed and healed.

May I never run away from the one face
that will always look on me tenderly.

Here I am, my God,
with a hundred little thoughts
going in a hundred different directions.

Teach me to be still
and to notice Your loving eyes on me.
Through Your love I will come to see
who I am and what I seek.
Teach my heart to listen to Your voice,
and refresh me with the touch
of Your strong and tender love.

As my eyes wander to Your gifts all around me,
may my heart never leave its true home with You.

On a Busy, Busy Day

Today is a busy, busy day,
with no time to stop and catch my breath.

Grant me the wisdom to find
peace in the midst of toil,
joy in the midst of stress,
humor in the midst of tension,
and to be aware of Your love.

I know that You think of me every moment.
I know that I cannot be lost to Your sight.
Direct my heart and my steps
that I may love and serve You in all I do.

In my struggle to achieve much,
may I not lose sight
of what is essential and everlasting.

Help me to remember that I can do more
in five minutes of calm
than in five hours of fury.

I bow before Your presence,
and start the day in peace;
for You are always at my side,
and nothing is too small or too hard for You.

How Do I Picture You?

To You, My Father

As I walk through the world, Father,
I feel a thrill:
it is Your world, and I am at home everywhere!

You thought of me, Father,
before I ever knew of You,
ages before my birth.
You created this universe,
this fantastic fairyland,
for me to play in and to grow in.

What makes You so giving, my God?
What urges You to move out in love
to us, who have nothing to give You?
What makes You love us—except love itself?

Love is Your name, Father,
tender compassion Your strength.
You show Your power by giving life.
You are too great to need our gifts,
but You invite us to love You,
so that our joy may be complete.

Fill me, then, to the brim
with Your goodness, Your wisdom and Your power.
With You at my side,
I will never be an orphan at life's banquet,
but a well-beloved child,
totally secure, deeply at home.

As I grow up, Father,
You wait for me to shed my childish dependence.
You invite me to be myself,
to think and question,
make mistakes and grow.
You would rather see me walking and falling
than see me stay still, afraid of falling.
My growth thrills You.
How could it ever displease You?

You invite me to keep growing,
ask questions,
explore Your world,
and find answers for myself.

Thank You for Your trust, Father!
Thank You for leaving Your world in our hands!
Hold our hand when we are frightened of life.
Teach us to love one another
as Your dear sons and daughters.
Pardon us for forgetting that we are Your children,
and treating Your world as though we had made it.

Correct us when we need it.
Frighten us into good sense—when you have to!
Secure in Your love,
we will walk through Your great, lovely world,
heads held high, hearts united in love,
hands busy doing what You ask us to do.

And one day, when this passing show is over,
we will reach Home, and gather around You.
We will shout and dance and sing and celebrate,
lost in wonder at all that You have prepared for us.
You will look into my eyes,
and I will know,
as I have never known before,
what it means to be truly at home.

To You, My Mother

Gentle Mother,
strong and tender,
let me sit beside You.
Let me drop from my weary shoulders
the burdens life has put on them—
work and worry, power and struggle,
and the incessant rush to prove myself.

Before You, Mother, I am wholly secure.
There is nothing I need to prove,
nothing I need to fear.
You are the one love that I need not win,
the one heart that will never disown me.

When I am weak, You give me strength.
When I falter, You steady my steps.
Falling, I have been raised up times without number.
The less I liked myself,
the more You reached out to me.

In the midst of confusion,
You are my one harbor of safety.
In the battle of life,
when I come to You wounded and frightened,
You are always there for me.
In my sin and shame,
You stand by my side,

against my sin and evil,
but never against me.

How can I thank You for such unspeakable
    tenderness?
How can I ever repay such a tremendous debt?

Pressing me to Your heart,
You whisper words that only mothers can say:
There are no debts, You say,
nothing to pay back, nothing to cancel.
My joy is Your joy; this is all You seek—
my complete happiness, now and forever.

I am speechless before love such as this.
It is far, far beyond my grasp.
My words, Mother, are stuck in my throat.
With tears of joy,
I press closer to You.
I lean my head on Your great heart—
the heart that will always be my home.

These tears are my best prayer, Mother—
tears of gratitude, tears of peace,
tears of deep and complete healing.
Hold me close to You till I am totally healed;
help me to be all that You want me to be.

To You, My Friend

Dearest friend, can we spend a while together?
With You I feel free and at home.
I can just be myself, without ceremony or pretense.
I can relax, I feel accepted,
and I know that whatever I say interests You.
You are my best and truest friend,
the one who has always stood by me.
You know me as I really am,
and You love me as no one else does.

You have shown me my beauty and worth,
and taught me to believe in myself.
You have seen good in me
when I myself didn't see it.
You pointed out my mistakes to me,
but never condemned or shamed me.

Thank You, best of friends, for the lovely times
    together.
Thank You for the freedom
with which I can treat You.
Thank You for meeting me at my level,
so that I never feel small or insignificant.

I feel blessed to be called Your friend,
Your companion, in whom You confide.
What greater honor than to enjoy Your friendship?
How can I thank You for Your divine playfulness?

For playful You are, never condescending,
never spiteful, nor given to vengeance.
You do not treat me as I truly deserve;
no, You treat me far above my merit.

I bring to this friendship my sincere desire
to be true, open and willing to change.
You bring Yourself, with Your ocean of gifts,
and You never stop giving, my good, prodigal friend!
I give You what I have—though that, too, is Your gift:
my heart, my love and my free decision
to listen to You and to be like You.

Make me, then, more like You
that I may become
a prodigal friend who loves without counting the cost.

To You, My Love

I never see enough of You, my love.
I want to see You, feel You, touch You.
I want to hold You; I want to be held.
Oh, I would give anything to be with You always!

My heart, my senses, my body—
every cell, every fiber of my being—
everything in me wants You, needs Your touch.
Why do You hide from me?
Why do You stay far away?

You awakened my heart to beauty and love.
Through pleasure and pain, light and darkness,
You led me to love You,
to give myself in joy.
I have surrendered myself—
everything I have, everything I am,
everything I will ever become.
All that I can ever possess
seems little compared to Your love.

What can the world give me
that can compare with Your love?
What is more precious than love's infinite passion?
To be with You is my greatest delight.
I would give the world to have a glimpse of You.

Come, endless love, take possession of me.
Make me one with You forever.
Listen to my heart;
see my longing.
Do not stay far off; for without You I die.

I cast off all that comes between us—
my fear, my sins, my attachments, my folly,
even my thoughts about You.
Stripped of everything but my desire for You,
I ask You to take me as I am.
Naked, I await love's embrace.

Gentle lover, passionate and tender,
You have loved me with an everlasting love.
You have loved me into being,
loved me into loving,
loved me unto folly.
Give me a love like Yours—
a love stronger than death,
a love deeper than myself.

Oh, no!
That is not enough for me!
Pour out Your own love into my heart!
Love in me and through me!

With Your love filling me, moving me,
I will love You back with Your own passion.
I will be an empty reed
which You fill with Your music.
Your love will purify me for love.
It will consume everything in me that is not love.
Through me—yet in spite of me—
You will reach out and love everyone,
everywhere, every day.

And when love will have charred
the trash of my little self,
the "I" I once knew will be gone,
and I will have found myself for the first time.

To You, My All

How do I picture You,
my God without name or face,
how do I tell myself who You are?

You are not one of the persons I meet,
not an idea, not an image,
not a part, however noble.
No, You are everything, in everything, in everyone.
You envelope us all in a mantle of love;
we are not lost to Your sight even for an instant.

You are more intimate than any human lover,
more present to my inmost self than I myself am.
These thoughts I think,
these words I form,
are but a shadow of Your thoughts of me,
Your words to my heart.

You move me from within to seek Your face.
You go ahead of me and wait for me.
You await me at every turn
with surprises only love can prepare.

You are the pure mountain spring,
the source of our love and our giving,
of colors and sounds, and all that we enjoy.
You lead me skillfully and surely, my tremendous
   lover,

to both ecstasy and peace—
and You remain hidden.

You hide Your face behind a thousand disguises
to give me the joy of discovering You anew.
And just as I begin to think I have caught You,
You show Yourself to me in more wondrous ways.

Playful Mystery, Tormenting Question,
Ecstatic Silence, my heart's Beloved,
who are You?
Where are You?
How do I picture You? How do I talk of You?

I will throw my words to the wind.
No need have I for special settings,
seasons and moods;
for You are not sealed off from life.
No, Your presence fills everything we touch.
You cannot forget us or be far away,
even when we think we are far from home.

This light is too much for my eyes,
this love too strong for my cowardice.
I am used to bits and pieces;
how do I take in what the universe cannot contain?

You answer from deep within me
and teach me this loving contradiction:
that I am greater than the world.
I will only be filled by You.

Come, then, my Joy, my All, my Everything!
Come and be everything in me.
Let all that is in me rise in welcome,
and receive the fullness for which I was made.

To You, My God

To know You as God
is to know
that we do not know You.
For You are immeasurably beyond
what we say or grasp.

You Surprised Me

Thoughts of a Skeptic

I won't be taken in
by any pious jargon.
I'll only admit what I can see or prove.

I have a healthy suspicion
toward words and gestures
by which some people claim
they are talking to God.
Aren't they deceiving themselves—
and perhaps others?

How can we be sure
we are talking to "God"?
How much is certain?
What can we know?

Won't we be better off
without religious dogma,
fanatic rivalries and
crazy claims to know it all?
Who will ever referee
the matches—and the brawls—
between self-appointed messengers
who speak for the Almighty?

No, I will have no part
in all this mumbo jumbo.
I will stick to the harder road
of reason, and of silence.

May I have nothing to do
with a self-righteous piety that condemns,
with narrowness that teaches hate,
and with ignorance that would claim
I am a cut above the rest.

Oh, no!
If there is a God—
I don't say there isn't one—
may He save us from all devotion
that takes us away from our tasks.
May He show us that it is we
who need each other's care and concern—
not He.
May He become a flame
that burns our selfish idols.
May He (She, It—whatever name we give God)
goad us to action, not to evasion.

May we find sacredness in persons,
not in things,
and use religion to grow,
not to stay childish.

May we be large-hearted and creative
like the Creator we claim to worship.
May I not toil and pray
to build up a bank account with God,
but rather let go
and share my gifts in service.
May we preserve our sense of limit,
and never claim to know
more than we really know.

May we have the good sense
not to feel superior,
just because some of us believe
we have got it all.

Oh, no, my God,
I'd rather die a skeptic
than claim to be
another's infallible guru,
or Your unerring mouthpiece.

The Angel and the Beast

I was walking down
the corridor of my heart
when I saw them—
saw them locked in combat.

It was an awe-inspiring sight.
It shook me.

I saw the angel of light,
all love, all joy, utter goodness,
locked in combat
with a hideous beast,
its features contorted
by arrogance and greed.

I could not take my eyes away.
Behind the strange spectacle,
something felt familiar—
vaguely yet deeply familiar.

And then I saw it—
and what I saw shook me to my bones.
Both the angel and the beast
had the same features.
Behind the ecstatic angelic look
and the contorted sneer of evil
was the same face—
my face!

Oh, my God,
I am both an angel of light
and the breeding nest of evil.
I am the heart where Christ and Buddha are born;
I am the pit where forces of evil gather.
My destiny is infinitely loftier than I thought;
I carry both heaven and hell within me.
What unbounded oceans I hold—
a sea of good and a sea of evil!
I can rise to the most sublime heights
or sink to unthinkable depravity.

O save me, save me from my own darkness,
from hidden whirlpools of cruelty and greed.
May I never let evil triumph in me;
may the demon never conquer the angel.

Your guiding hand waits to help me,
to mold me in goodness, in love, in joy.
You long to make me like You,
a ray of Your light, Your peace, Your compassion.

You have put Your seal upon my heart;
I remain Yours forever.
Let me never give in to evil.
Let me not become a heap of garbage,
when I can be a brilliant star.

Oh, what a divine lineage is mine!
I am Your image, Your child, Your very own.
I excel the stars in brightness,
for You live deep within my heart.

And yet,
and yet,
I can sink incredibly lower.
I can smear Your image with filth.

I can lock love out, entertain hate,
and breed monsters where angels were to be born.

Oh, help me, heal me, steady my heart!
I am too much for me to handle!
My greatness fascinates and frightens me.
I am a riddle waiting to be solved—
to be solved over and over again.
I am a question, a mystery, a labyrinth.
I am both messiah and tyrant, deliverer and prison.
I am both Christ and Judas,
loving avatar and treacherous betrayer.
The righteous Rama and the insolent Ravana
are both my kin.
Oh, save me from the pits I myself dig!
Lead me to the shore of love's gentle light.
All through my earthly journey,
this deadly combat goes on.
All the holiness I venerate in shrines,
and all the evils I decry in the world,
are found right here—in my heart.
I can be the saviour of the world,
or the root of its rot.

I take Your hand and lay it on my head.
I seek Your guiding light.
Your power is greater than my struggle;
no evil pull is a match for Your love.

Trusting You, I go forth to face the day.
I will choose truth over lies;
compassion over cowardice.
Justice and mercy I will serve.

Oh, may I be the child of light I am called to be.
May divine power break through the darkness.

May good triumph in superabundant measure,
and turn me into an angel of light.

In the battlefield of my heart,
in the decisions I take today,
I want goodness to be the winner.

I want that to happen right now,
in the very next decision I take.

Help me;
show me how.

The Mystic and the Skeptic

There is a mystic within me,
as well as a skeptic.
They are both real—
and both are me.

I hear them talking, arguing,
at times fighting.
I can't yet decide who is stronger.

The skeptic calls the mystic blind;
and the mystic hurls back, "You are deaf!"

Right here, within my heart,
are a blind musician
and a deaf critic.

The mystic is a musician, a poet;
he hears melodies the skeptic misses.
He hears sounds, harmonies,
the travail of all creation—but he is blind.

The skeptic is an eagle-eyed questioner.
Oh, how sharp his sight is!
He sees, he questions, he takes things apart;
without him I would be fooled and misled.
But—isn't it sad?—he is stone deaf!

For him a dance is an absurd sight,
a senseless waste of energy,

a purposeless flinging of limbs—
for he misses the melodies people dance to.

Blind musician, hearer of melodies;
deaf scientist, critical observer—
I am both.

No wonder I feel torn.
Should I trust my feel for oneness,
or suspect all unexamined answers?
Shall I reach beyond reason into the silence,
or wait cautiously till I see clearly?

If I am all trust, I would become a doormat.
Unquestioned certainties would turn me into a
    fanatic.
But if I seek proofs that cannot be shaken,
almost nothing can be enjoyed.
There is so little in life that can really be "proved."

Shall I follow the melody,
or analyze and explore?
Shall I be a mystic or a skeptic?
If only I could be both!

Are You amused at the goings-on
in the arena of my heart?
Why did You make me half-mystic, half-skeptic?
Why did You give me both passion and a cool head?

Teach me to combine Your gifts in wisdom—
to soar like an eagle,
but without forgetting the earth;
and to follow the melodies,
with no fear of questions.
Teach me how to feel and think,
ask questions and be silent.
Teach me to embrace life and dance to its melody,
while keeping my eyes open to avoid pitfalls.

May the mystic never blind me
to the real needs of creatures,
nor the skeptic make me deaf
to the voice of the Creator.

Thank You for my friends, the mystic and the skeptic.
I need them both.
I do not want to be deaf; nor do I love blindness.
Keep me listening to both,
that I may be fully human—
a passionate lover with a calm, discerning mind,
and a dispassionate seer, fired by an inner melody.

Teach me, Friend and Lover,
to be a skeptic before easy answers,
and a mystic who hears the silent melody.

I'm Afraid of You!

Are You disappointed
that I'm afraid of You?

In spite of Your incessant care,
after untold signs of Your love,
I still hesitate.
I hold back.

I fear surrendering to Your Love.
I'm afraid You'll ask me too much.
I'm afraid You will want me
to let go of what I love,
of what I cherish most.

Will You ask me
to give up my dear ones?
Will You think I am too attached to them?
Do You want the sacrifice of my friends?
Do You plan to break my heart?

What about the things I have—
my house, my work, my money, my possessions?
You know what they mean to me;
some of them have cost me so much.

And then the precious intangible treasures—
popularity and fame, freedom and prestige;
and, yes, my health, my senses, my mind,
my strength, my memory, my dreams . . .

Surrender is an easy word;
it really calls for a crucifixion.
How can You ask me to surrender?
You remind me that one day I'll have to let go.
True—but death seems far away; far, far away.

You tell me You know my heart's desires,
that only You can fill me as I dream.
Did my mother crush me when she held me?
Did my father let me fall
when I jumped into his arms?

I ought to know
that You are father and mother;
that Your tender care far exceeds all human love.
But I still hesitate; I fear.
I'm afraid of the unknown.

Hold me tenderly and speak to my heart.
Show me where I will find rest.
A part of me knows
that what I call loss is supreme gain;
that my apparent freedom is slavery.
My gain and my loss
are the opposite of what selfish fear tells me.

And yet, I am afraid.

Does a child in the womb
fear being born?
Would it be mercy to keep it
forever in the womb?
No, it was conceived to be born,
to face a new world, and grow.

Hold me, then, as I move forward in trust,
as I throw myself into Your arms.
Lead my frightened heart to the peace it seeks.
Let me delay no longer.

I trust;
I come;
I surrender.
I surrender my fear, my clinging, my possessions—
all that I am, all that I'll ever have.

Everything in me is Your gift to me;
let me not stop growing
by clinging to what I have.

Take me as I am, as I offer You myself.
Whatever You do is the best I can have;
for You know my heart's desires better than I do.

In Your hands is my life;
In Your heart lies my destiny.
Where would I be more secure?

You Surprised Me!

I began to talk to You in different moods and seasons,
looking for answers, seeking hope and comfort.
I thought You would draw nearer to me
and give me the answers I wanted from You.

Along the way, You surprised me.
You are not the helper I thought You were.
You did not move closer; You cannot come nearer,
for You are closer to me than I am to myself.

But something else changed—
here is the second surprise!
I am not the person I thought I knew.
I am an unknown land still to be discovered,
a mystery too deep for me.
I have not even begun to see
who I am, who I really am,
or what fascinating treasures lie buried within me.

Over these silent hours, our roles have been reversed.
You are the revealer, and I the one who listens.
The gift is from You to me;
I need only let go and receive.
I need not speak, or ask, or remind You.
All You ask me is to be,
to stand before You and be loved.

Oh, what unspeakable love is this!
It is folly by all human standards.
I do not know how I can thank You.

Your offer sounds too good to be true,
far too generous for me to fathom.

May I never shrink before this cascade!
May I choose to see, to trust, to receive.

May the "I" I cling to, die and rise again,
and become the fullness You hold out to me.

Questions People Ask

Why pray? After all, God knows our needs and does not need to be informed.

Perfectly true.

"God" is a human word to indicate the Holy Mystery that envelopes us totally, the one Presence to which nothing comes as information or as a surprise. God does not come to know; God knows. All that exists, all that goes on in my complicated little head, is, of course, present to God in utter transparency.

It is we who need reminders, information, gentle (or high pressure) persuasion; not God.

Prayer, therefore, is not an attempt to inform God of what is happening, nor, much less, an arrogant effort to suggest better courses of action ("God, listen to me; I'll tell You what to do!"). It is not, thirdly, "supernatural lobbying"—trying to make God better disposed through our pleading and our cleverly worded praise!

What, then, is prayer? Why should we pray at all?

Prayer is awareness.
Prayer is acceptance.
Prayer is the radical willingness to be changed.

Radical willingness to be changed?

Yes.
If we mean by prayer the special moments we set

147

apart to talk to—or listen to—the Loving Heart of reality we call God, it is simply to open our hearts and hands to receive what Infinite Love is longing to give us. It is not a question of our asking for ten, hoping to receive at least two; it is rather the case of our asking for ten, and then realizing that our dreams are too small, our requests too timid, our hopes too narrow—that God was waiting to give us much more.

In prayer, a change of perspective takes place. The narrowness of our vision gives way to the largeness of Love's outpouring generosity. Divine liberality waits for us to be ready to receive—to receive more than we deserve or expect.

True prayer, therefore, is essentially simple: the willingness to let go, to be transformed, to be open to receive.

Who, then, is a prayerful or religious person?

The "prayerful" person is not necessarily one who "says" many prayers, but rather the person who is ready to be surprised by grace.

Such a person is willing to be challenged by the Divine, that is, by life, by people, by events—by any voice God may choose to use to get our attention.

Such a person perceives himself or herself more and more as a gift; as a cherished someone who matters.

Love invites him out.

Love invites me out?

Yes. We dare to move out of fear into the paths of love, not out of a moral compulsion or the burden of induced guilt, but because we feel ourselves treasured and supported by Endless Love. We become more and more aware of how much we receive, and how capable we are of giving. We see ourselves as significant links in God's chain of giving.

How do I know if I am praying well?

How do you know if you love well? How do you know if you are a good driver?

The true lover's attention is on the beloved; not on one's activity of loving.

The really accomplished driver is almost one with the vehicle; one's attention is not on a series of steps learned by heart and executed rigidly.

Similarly, progress in prayer may be best indicated by a shift in focus—from self-doubt, techniques of prayer, and analysis of degrees and results, to a self-transcending vision and concern. If prayer has changed us, our heart and our eyes look on the world as God's world—with love and compassion, with courage and serenity. Our fidelity is not to an activity called prayer (or prayers), but to the mysterious presence that beckons to us in our stillness. This voice creates our unique history. In responding to it we discover what it means to be free.

Is not all this talk about "God" and "prayer" mostly psychological help? In what we call "prayer," are we not merely playing with our own words and fantasies?

Psychology? That needs some explanation. When twentieth century men and women (especially the more literate and academically oriented) use words like "psychology" or "psychological," the reference is to the whole realm of human emotions, needs, thought processes, conditioning and behavior patterns, as well as to the currently acclaimed explanations of such experiences. Each epoch of human history, every major culture, has had its favorite paradigms for talking about human life. Ours seems to like "psychological" interpretations.

What about a psychological understanding of prayer? Is prayer some kind of self-talk, using fantasies taken from one's personal history and cultural setting?

To some degree, it certainly is.

Prayer does use fantasies about a powerful, loving parent figure (or friend) who is there to help me.

It does soothe troubled minds with special reassurances.

And it does have "psychological" effects: peace, harmony, strength, a sense of dignity and purpose, the willingness to get over hurts and move on to better things.

Whether these assurances and effects are illusory or not cannot be tested by the sciences; for the Reality they refer to lies beyond human testing.

Aren't counseling and psychotherapy a better substitute for religious practices?

Let us see.

Are the believer and the therapist saying the same things when they use words like "peace," "faith," "hope," "helping" or "healing"?

To a limited extent, yes.

To a much larger degree, no.

Just as the words "I love" can mean very different things when spoken by a child, a lover, a doting parent, a flatterer or a gourmet (about food!), so too, most words referring to personal experiences stand for a vast gamut of experiences. The words "I care for you" can mean very different things when uttered by different people. Similarly, "I am healed!" or "Oh, what joy!" referring to a deep experience of personal transformation, are worlds apart from the same words in a setting of physical health or meeting a likable person.

We do not have adequate tools to measure the different meanings—or to compare them.

What can be studied—and needs to be—is the emotional and social "fallout" of prayer. Does it make a person more "human"—that is, more poised, more positive, more loving, more open to life, more realistic? Or does it deepen a person's unhealthy urges—excessive fear, crippling guilt, self-righteousness, or flight from life?

Such an inquiry on the part of the therapeutic sciences would be a valid service to everyone concerned—to those who pray, to those who are confused about prayer, and especially to those who seem to hear conflicting messages from their humanity and from their "God."

For whatever our (necessarily imperfect) religious upbringing may tell us, the true God cannot ask us to turn against ourselves, or to be insensitive to our deepest desires.

What do I gain if I pray? What do I stand to lose if I don't?

Gain? Loss? What do these words mean?

What do we "gain" if we watch the sunset, or spend time with friends, or take time for intimacy? What do we "lose" if we are never hugged by a loved one or discuss nothing more serious than the weather—or money?

There is no way to calculate the gain and the loss in gold and silver, added income or social mobility. What we are talking about is that mysterious reality called quality—the quality of our life, the way we choose to live our human life.

People who learn to listen to the deep part of themselves—to the radiant Presence the mystics speak of—notice a new sense of purpose, a new energy and optimism, the capacity to enjoy everyday things in a uniquely joyful way. They feel very inadequate if called upon to put their experiences into words, but others who know them notice in their persons something more than healthy skin and superficial charm and clever humor.

You probably have come across such radiant persons, and wondered what their secret is.

Better still, you probably have had such special moments yourself and caught sight of the Mysterious Other who addresses you in words you cannot repeat.

If so, you will know what I am trying to say through these ill-chosen words. You will have noticed that my attempt to describe your experience resembled a child's attempts to create a castle with pebbles on the beach.

What is the use of books like this one?

To free you to be yourself.

To tell you it is all right to talk to God—to address your mystery—in any way you find meaningful.

To free you, perhaps, from the burden of some prejudices about prayer.

To remind you that the center of attention—the center of God's attention—is not prayer, but you.

Me?

Yes!

The fascinating unknown you will get to know in prayer is the world's most mysterious marvel—yourself. The real you—not the mannequin described by fashion, or the cog in the wheel used for production, or a number in the national statistics.

You are the great unknown land full of surprises waiting to be discovered.

The sure Guide who will lead you in this exploration is God.

For God—and God alone—knows this territory fully. And God's "guided tour" of your mysterious universe is prayer.

What you have just asked is itself a wonderful prayer: Teach me to pray!

The Divine Presence within you will lead you on your unique, individual path, to splendors you have not yet seen, to surprises you cannot imagine, to truths you do not yet grasp.

Your God will meet you each day at the level at which you find yourself, and show you to yourself in a new light.

You will discover that you have lights and energies and spiritual resources you did not suspect.

You will be led.

Paradoxically, in letting yourself be led, you will discover your true inner freedom, your truest identity as a human being.

For we discover our humanity when—and to the degree—we get caught up in the absolute, unutterable mystery we call "God."

How do I start?

Very simply, by talking to this Presence, this Friend, this Lover (or this Tormenting Question) in any words you may choose.

Or by being still, and listening.

Or by noticing that you are unable to be still, to be silent, and paying attention to the "crowds" that people your mind.

Allow your God-given capacity for wonder, for silence, for love, to flourish.

There is more to life than what you have seen so far; very much more than any of us can understand.

You need not wait for privileged moments or special settings. This present moment is as good as any other. (And it is all you have; the rest is fantasy.)

Start, if you like, right now.

Talk to God.

You will find, to your surprise, that you knew how to, all the while.

You will perhaps begin with a feeling of entering a strange foreign land; but, as you walk on, you will notice that you are really coming home.

For home is where our truest self resides, and we get to know our truest self only by entering the kingdom of mystery.

It is time for me to withdraw.

The setting is not one of good-bye, but of gazing with hope in the same direction.

We will meet—as we were meant to meet—in a region beyond words and shadows, in that radiant silence that gives meaning to all our words.

In that silence we do not part; we find each other.

For we will have shed the disguise that hides our true
    face.

Close the book, then, and enter.

You are not alone; you have come home.

ABOUT THE AUTHOR

Joe Mannath, S.D.B., is dean of the Department of Philosophy at Sacred Heart College in Madras, India, and a Visiting Professor, Chair in Christianity, at the University of Madras. He has taught and conducted workshops on philosophy, human relations, and spirituality. Versed in several languages, including English, Italian, German, and Spanish, Father Mannath has had a distinguished career and personal experience in settings as diverse as Boston and Madras, Oxford and Rome, Cambridge and Poona.